NOMINATING PRESIDENTS

Recent Titles in
Contributions in Political Science

NOMINATING PRESIDENTS

An Evaluation of Voters and Primaries

John G. Geer

FOREWORD BY
James W. Davis

Contributions in Political Science, Number 236
Bernard K. Johnpoll, *Series Editor*

GREENWOOD PRESS
New York · Westport, Connecticut · London

TECHNICAL COLLEGE OF THE LOWCOUNTRY
LEARNING RESOURCES CENTER
POST OFFICE BOX 1288 *0 26158*
BEAUFORT, SOUTH CAROLINA 29901-1288

Library of Congress Cataloging-in-Publication Data

Geer, John Gray.
    Nominating presidents : an evaluation of voters and primaries /
John G. Geer.
       p. cm.—(Contributions in political science, ISSN 0147-1066 ;
  no. 236)
    Bibliography: p.
    Includes index.
    ISBN 0-313-26182-2 (lib. bdg. : alk. paper)
    1. Presidents—United States—Nomination. 2. Primaries—United
States. I. Title. II. Series.
JK522.G44 1989
324.5'4'0973—dc20   89-2130

British Library Cataloguing in Publication Data is available.

Library of Congress Catalog Card Number: 89-2130
ISBN: 0-313-26182-2
ISSN: 0147-1066

First published in 1989

Greenwood Press, Inc.
88 Post Road West, Westport, Connecticut 06881

Printed in the United States of America

∞

The paper used in this book complies with the
Permanent Paper Standard issued by the National
Information Standards Organization (Z39.48-1984).

10 9 8 7 6 5 4 3 2 1

Copyright Acknowledgments

Grateful acknowledgment is given for permission to use material first published in the
article "Assessing the Representativeness of Electorates in Presidential Primaries" by John
G. Geer in *The American Journal of Political Science*, Vol. 32, No. 4, November 1988,
pp. 929–945. The journal is published by the University of Texas Press.

Additional thanks are extended for permission to use material first published in the article
"Rules Governing Presidential Primaries," also by John G. Geer, in *The Journal of Poli-
tics*, Vol. 48, No. 4, November 1986, pp. 1006–1025. This journal is also published by the
University of Texas Press.

To Maria,
with love

Contents

Figures and Tables

FIGURES

TABLES

Foreword

Twenty years ago the study of presidential primaries was a neglected area of American politics. Only one book on the subject had been published since Louise Overacker's pioneering study in 1926. The explanation for this academic indifference was simple: presidential primaries did not then play a major role in the presidential nominating process.

Until 1972, presidential nominees were almost always the choice of state party leaders and insiders. Only fifteen states permitted rank-and-file voters to select delegates to the national conventions, and most of the primaries were advisory in nature; that is, the delegates were not legally bound to vote for the winner of the primary. But this is now all changed.

The post–1968 Democratic party reforms, indirectly at least, triggered the rapid spread of presidential primaries across the land. By 1980, roughly 35 state legislatures had adopted some form of presidential primary, sponsored originally by the Progressive movement early in the twentieth century. Moreover, because these laws tightened the link between delegate pledges and the individual presidential candidate, the candidate could now count on pledged delegates to support his candidacy as long as he remained in contention. Chiefly as a result of these two reforms the nomination decision has been taken out of the hands of the party elite and given to the mass electorate. Clearly, the road to the White House is now via the presidential primaries. Indeed, the nominee in the out-party (the party that does not control the White House) has, since 1972, invariably been the victor in the primaries. Also, all three incumbent presidents seeking reelection since then have clinched renomination by winning the primaries, though President Ford barely nosed out former California governor Ronald Reagan in 1976.

With this rapid shift in the way presidential candidates have been nominated since 1972, it is not surprising that a host of books and articles on the subject have appeared in print.

John G. Geer, author of this study, is a rising young scholar who has carefully analyzed the effects of presidential primaries on the nominating process. He is among the first to provide a systematic in-depth evaluation of primary voters and their qualifications for picking party nominees. His research shows that primary voters are more like general election voters than earlier findings by Austin Ranney and others have shown.

Geer addresses such major topics as the so-called "unrepresentativeness" of primary voters, the level of primary voter turnout, the role of the mass media, and the effect of the various delegate allocation systems on the type of nominee selected. Whether or not one agrees with his conclusions, the reader will find that Geer's analysis deserves close scrutiny. To correct some of the flaws he sees in the existing system Geer offers a number of proposed reforms: a system of grouped or regional primaries; preference voting in which voters list their first, second, and third choices for president; a 25-percent set-aside of national convention delegates for party leaders; and proportional allocation of delegates to reflect voter choice in the primaries.

Geer, to his credit, does not advocate a national primary. Deceptively appealing, a national primary suffers from a number of serious shortcomings, and Geer offers convincing evidence why this drastic reform should not be adopted. Geer prefers to keep the national convention as the official mechanism for selecting the nominee. His proposed reforms would leave intact the national convention's functions of selecting a vice-presidential nominee, serving as the rallying point for the national party, a forum to write a party platform, a proven means to heal party wounds after bitter primary fights, and an opportunity for the 50 state parties to help the nominee organize and kick off the general election campaign.

Critics may differ over one of the most provocative aspects of Geer's regional primary plan. Geer proposes to include both New England and five Southeastern states in the same regional primary. His purpose is to achieve an ideological and population balance within the region. Similarly, he proposes to include Minnesota, North Dakota, Texas, and Louisiana in the same Middle Plains regional primary for the same reasons. How saleable this proposal would be is open to question, but it merits the reader's thoughtful consideration.

To provide a more accurate measurement of voter sentiment in the primaries, Geer urges a preference ballot or "alternative vote" system. By allowing voters to register their first, second, and third choices, Geer believes that the candidates selected would enjoy broader popular support than the present system of aggregating only first preferences. Preference balloting, he feels, would prevent extremist candidates with a narrow constituency from capturing a plurality nomination, while moderate, mainstream candidates kill off each other in the primaries. Though Geer argues that the public could be persuaded to buy preference voting, many skeptics, including the present writer, are inclined to believe that the complicated ballot-marking system would create more problems for the voter than it would solve. Nevertheless, the reader should profit immeasurably from evaluating Geer's carefully drafted reforms.

Greenwood Press should also be commended for publishing another first-rate study of the presidential primary system—certainly the most convoluted, complex, and fascinating national leadership selection process of all the Western democracies.

James W. Davis
Western Washington University

Preface

The idea for this book took root in Stanley Kelley's seminar on party politics in the spring of 1982. During that term I began to read about both the present and past arrangements for nominating presidents. This strategy afforded me the opportunity to read not only the work of political scientists like James Ceasar, William Crotty, Nelson Polsby, and Austin Ranney, but also scholars like James Bryce, Woodrow Wilson, M. Ostrogorski, and Edward Sait. Much to my surprise, *every* nominating system since the inception of the Constitution has come under attack by political observers of the time. Interestingly, a common theme of those attacks was that the decision-makers, whether congressmen, party leaders, or the rank and file, were not qualified to choose presidential nominees. There were generally two problems with these claims. First, many of the arguments (both past and present) lacked a sound empirical foundation. Second, these criticisms appeared often to be motivated by partisan considerations. So, for instance, one reason local politicians viewed the congressional caucus as "unrepresentative" was that members of Congress, not these local officials, were nominating presidential candidates.

The following pages have two objectives that I hope begin to develop answers to whether the current set of decision-makers, voters in primaries, are qualified to choose presidential nominees. The first objective is to develop standards to judge the qualifications of voters in primaries. This task is fraught with pitfalls because any number of standards might be deemed reasonable by political scientists. I have tried to give good reasons for my particular criteria, but I am sure some will take issue with them. Such criticism will surely be justified, but the more important issue is to encourage scholars to think explicitly about the standards we use to assess those who select our presidential nominees. If I accomplish that, this book will have been well worth the effort.

The second objective is to provide a body of systematic information about voters in primaries. Until recently there has been a lack of good data concerning voters in primaries. But because of the efforts of people in the National Elections Studies and individuals like Thomas Patterson, more and more data have become available. With such data we can learn more about the behavior of voters in primaries and thus be more sure of our generalizations about them.

This project began at Princeton University. While the work has changed greatly since then, I still owe many thanks to the people there. First, I want to express my appreciation to members of Research Services at Princeton University. Doug Mills and Shirley Robbins provided invaluable assistance with the statistical packages. Judith Rowe provided me almost unlimited computer time, an office to work in, and easy access to much of the data for this study. Each of these people made my life a lot more enjoyable as I labored through the early stages of the project.

I also want to extend my appreciation to Tom Cronin and Fred Greenstein for reading early drafts of the manuscript. Their comments and encouragement were greatly appreciated.

I especially want to thank those who helped guide this project in its initial phases. Tom Rochon provided many useful comments and much sound advice. He was always willing to read and talk about my written work. I shall always remember his help and friendship. John Zaller, through his insightful remarks, helped strengthen this manuscript. John frequently found just the right wording of a sentence that helped clarify an idea. Jim DeNardo also supplied excellent advice, always managing to find new ways to look at the data. He also had a knack for organizing my arguments more effectively than I had. In each case, his efforts made the book better.

In particular, I want to thank Stanley Kelley. Not only was he my best critic, but he helped me to understand politics and how one might fruitfully study it. Whatever is of value in this study can be attributed in large part to his efforts. I owe him a debt that cannot be repaid. I shall always remember his patience, time, and perhaps most important, his friendship.

Since I have moved from the ivy to the desert, a number of people have assisted my reworking of this book. Larry Bartels read an earlier draft of the manuscript and supplied some very useful comments. Warren Miller also provided valuable assistance on some of my chapters. Ruth Jones, my chair at Arizona State University, created a nice environment to work in, which allowed me to rewrite the entire manuscript more quickly that I might have otherwise. The College of Liberal Arts at ASU provided me a grant to help fund the later stages of the project. Finally, I would like to thank Pat Kenney. Pat's comments on my written work were of great value. But even more important, our many conversations about the nominating process helped clarify and sharpen my thinking on the subject. I greatly appreciated his willingness to share his time and ideas.

The Inter-university Consortium for Political and Social Research (ICPSR) also deserves a note of thanks. Much of the data used in this study were made available by the ICPSR. The consortium does not, however, bear any responsibility for the analyses and interpretations presented here.

Last, but not least, I would like to thank my wife, Maria. When she agreed to marry me, she probably was not aware that along with me came this project. Despite the old saying that "three is a crowd," Maria was always helpful and encouraging. It is for this reason I dedicate the book to her. Of course, with our 15-month-old daughter, Megan (and another child on the way), there is even greater reason to dedicate these pages to her.

Whatever good resides in this study can be attributed to the help of all these people. The faults that remain are purely my own.

John G. Geer
Tempe, Arizona

NOMINATING PRESIDENTS

═══ 1 ═══

Introduction

I don't care who does the electing, so long as I can do the nominating.
William "Boss" Tweed

This statement by the one-time leader of Tammany Hall underscores the importance of controlling the nominating process. While scholars and political pundits obviously care about "who does the electing," many agree with Tweed that nominating candidates is the more critical stage in the selection process. As William Keech and Donald Matthews (1976) succinctly observe, "presidential nominations are more important than presidential elections" (p. 1). Perhaps because the stakes are high, there have been frequent struggles during the course of American history over who gets to "do the nominating." Nearly one hundred and seventy years ago proponents of the congressional caucus were battling with those who advocated a system that gave state and local party leaders a greater voice in selecting presidential nominees. State and local party leaders won that battle, establishing a series of caucuses and a national party convention. Since the turn of the century, the struggle has been over whether party leaders or the rank and file should choose contenders for the Oval Office. Party leaders have had the upper hand during most of this time. But beginning in 1972 and continuing today, the rank and file have become the central decision-makers in the process. It is this latest change that is the subject of this book.

The most recent struggle, which has been going on for over 75 years, has focused largely on the merits of the direct primary. This delegate-selecting device first became part of the presidential nominating process in 1912.[1] Politicians, like Robert LaFollette and Woodrow Wilson, originally supported the adoption of primaries to wrestle control of nominations away from party bosses and give it to the rank and file. On the surface, at least, their effort was successful. By 1916, over 40 percent of the states relied on the direct primary to select delegates to the national party conventions (see Table 1.1). But despite the widespread use of primaries, party leaders retained control of presidential nominations.

Starting in 1948, however, individual primaries began to influence the outcome of some struggles for the presidential nomination (Davis 1980). The final decision still remained in the hands of the party leadership, but a good showing in a primary could greatly increase a contender's prospects. John Kennedy, for instance, boosted his chance of securing the nomination with a victory in the 1960 West Virginia primary. Barry Goldwater was able to fend off a challenge from Nelson Rockefeller by defeating him in the 1964 California primary. In 1952, Dwight Eisenhower's ability to win votes in primaries helped earn him the Republican nomination.

Overall, presidential primaries served mainly an advisory role to party leaders from 1912 to 1968. That is, if a candidate showed an ability to win votes in primaries, the party leadership might consider that evidence when selecting the nominee. But a series of victories in the primaries did not guarantee anything. For instance, in competitive races for the nomination, the top vote getter in the primaries became the nominee only about 40 percent of the time, showing that party leaders often ignored the advice offered by voters in primaries.[2]

In the 1970s, however, the influence of primaries grew dramatically and no longer served as just recommendations to the party leaders. As Table 1.1 shows, the number of primaries grew over 40 percent between 1968 and 1972. Overall, about 60 percent of the delegates from both parties were selected through direct primaries in 1972—an increase of over 50 percent from 1968. A majority of delegates were also selected by primaries in 1916 and 1920, but in 1972 the representatives to national conventions were committed to support particular candidates. This change meant that state and local party leaders lost control of their delegations. Primaries, therefore, became a dominant force in the presidential nominating system. This power is well illustrated by the fact that since 1972 nearly 90 percent of the nominees have also been the top vote getters in the primaries.[3] This proportion is more than double what it was during the 1912 to 1968 period.

Since primaries dominate the delegate selection process, citizens who participate in these events have become the central decision-makers in choosing the occupants of the White House. No longer can party leaders control the selection of candidates. This passing of the torch has re-

Table 1.1
The Influence of Presidential Primaries, 1912—1988

Year	Number of Primaries		Percent of Delegates		Percent of All Delegates
	Democratic	Republican	Democratic	Republican	Total
1912	12	13	32.9	41.7	37.3
1916	20	20	53.5	58.9	56.2
1920	16	20	44.6	57.8	51.2
1924	14	17	35.5	45.3	40.3
1928	17	16	42.2	44.9	43.5
1932	16	14	40.0	37.7	38.8
1936	14	12	36.5	37.5	37.0
1940	13	13	35.8	38.8	37.3
1944	14	13	36.7	38.7	37.7
1948	14	12	36.3	36.0	36.1
1952	15	13	38.7	39.0	38.8
1956	19	19	42.7	44.8	43.7
1960	16	15	38.3	38.6	38.5
1964	17	17	45.7	45.6	45.6
1968	15	15	40.2	38.1	39.1
1972	22	21	65.3	56.8	61.0
1976	30	30	76.0	71.0	73.5
1980	35	34	71.8	76.0	73.7
1984	25	30	62.1	71.0	66.1
1988	34	35	66.6	76.9	70.2

Source: Crotty and Jackson (1985), p. 16. Data for 1988 came from
Congressional Quarterly Weekly Report, February 27th, 1988, p. 532.

ceived, at best, mixed reviews from political scientists. Most students of American politics have been highly critical of this change, arguing the current arrangement yields poor candidates (see, for instance, Ceasar 1979, 1982; Polsby 1983; Keeter and Zukin 1983; Kirkpatrick 1978). Much of the blame for the system's inadequacies falls on the shoulders of voters in primaries. Many scholars view these participants as unrepresentative of the party rank and file, uninformed about the candidates, and too heavily influenced by the actions of the news media.

The purpose of this study is to examine systematically the criticisms leveled against voters in primaries. The results should shed some light on whether the public is capable of selecting good presidential candidates. A few scholars have been sympathetic to the increased influence of primaries (Crotty 1977, 1983; Nakamura and Sullivan 1978a, 1978b; Bode and Casey 1980; Nelson 1985), but none of them has explicitly assessed the qualifications of voters to select presidential nominees.

The first requirement to undertake this task is to secure data about voters in primaries. Fortunately, more and more data have become available over the last decade, making possible an in-depth examination of voters in primaries. In three of the last four presidential elections, panel studies have been conducted during the primaries—in 1976 by Thomas Patterson and in 1980 and 1988 by the National Election Studies (NES). In 1984, the NES also conducted the "continuous monitoring" survey, which polled cross sections of the electorate over the entire election year. In addition, a wealth of information lies in CBS/ *New York Times* and ABC/*Washington Post* exit polls of presidential primaries. Of course, one can also draw on Gallup Polls and various aggregate statistics for information about public opinion, turnout and allocation of delegates.[4]

While having an abundant supply of quality data is necessary, one must also develop standards to assess the criticisms of voters. This task, of course, is largely a normative enterprise. But without establishing clear benchmarks, one risks arriving at hasty or unreasonable conclusions. For instance, how does one distinguish between "informed" and "uninformed" voters? Or what constitutes a "representative" nominating system? Different standards can lead to different conclusions. Thus, to avoid potential confusion, I shall try to be explicit about the criteria I use to assess voters in primaries.

At this point I shall briefly sketch the criticisms to be addressed in this book. These paragraphs will highlight both the need to secure additional evidence about how voters in primaries behave and the need to create explicit standards to judge their qualifications to choose nominees.

RAISING DOUBTS ABOUT THE CONVENTIONAL WISDOM

One of the more common complaints about voters in primaries is that they are unrepresentative of the party following. The general view is that because of low turnout, more ideologically extreme voters have a disproportionate influence in primaries (Lengle 1981). As a result, the more moderate elements of the party lack a clear voice in the process. George McGovern's nomination is often cited as evidence that voters are unrepresentative, since the former senator from South Dakota was more ideologically extreme than most of his opponents in the primaries (Lengle 1981; Brams 1978; Kirkpatrick 1976). But Barry Goldwater, also an "extremist," was nominated under the pre-1972 system, and Jimmy Carter, Gerald Ford, George Bush, Ronald Reagan, and Michael Dukakis were not "extremists," yet they were nominated under the current arrangement, suggesting that the evidence for this claim is not as clear as some contend. To be sure of our claims, more evidence is needed. But before any data can be brought to bear, one needs to address the following question: Who should voters in primaries represent? All too often the question of representation is tackled without clearly specifying who are the "party following." Is it active members of the party organization? Nonvoters in primaries? Party identifiers? Or people who vote for the party in the general election? Different answers affect one's assessment of the representativeness of the system, suggesting that this matter needs further exploration both from an empirical and normative angle.

Another criticism of voters is that not enough participate in primaries (Davis 1980; Marshall 1981; Ceasar 1982). One of the central arguments in favor of primaries is that they open up the process to the rank and file. Yet the low rate of turnout suggests that many citizens do not take advantage of this opportunity. But what constitutes "low" turnout? The rate of participation appears low when compared with that in the general election, but is such a comparison fair? Would it be better to compare it to participation in caucuses? Even if turnout is low, does that mean that the electorate does not care about the process? Perhaps the rules governing primaries depress turnout, and it is not that voters lack interest in the process. We need, therefore, to develop good and clear benchmarks when deciding whether turnout is low or not.

The claim that voters in primaries are uninformed is another example of a possibly hasty conclusion. Voters certainly are not as well informed as party leaders, but are they as well informed as participants in other elections? We do not know. Is it reasonable to expect voters to be as well informed as party leaders? No one has addressed these questions. Scott Keeter and Cliff Zukin (1983) present data on how much information the electorate possesses about the candidates seeking the nomination and the relevant issues in the campaign. Yet without establishing any clear benchmarks to judge how well informed the electorate is, they conclude that voters know and learn "little about the candidates running for their party's nomination for president" (p. 112). But is such a conclusion fair without first establishing some standard of how informed voters should be? Larry Bartels (1988) and Henry Brady and Richard Johnston (1987) show that the electorate acquires information about the candidates as the process unfolds, suggesting that at least a few citizens learn about the contenders. Perhaps the rank and file are not as uninformed as we conventionally think. But in any case, we need to be clear about what constitutes an "informed" electorate.

The perception that voters in primaries are uninformed has led some experts to suggest that these participants make poor decisions. Thomas Marshall (1981) argues, for example, that "voters appear to search only long enough to find a candidate who appeals to them on a key issue or personality trait. Or some voters may find that there is only one candidate who does not offend them. A voter who perceives a particularly appealing candidate, or one who finds all but one candidate objectionable, then chooses that contender" (p. 141). Voters rely on this type of decision-making, according to Marshall, because they "often misunderstand candidates' issues stands" (p. 140). The picture painted by Marshall is hardly flattering of voters and does not inspire faith in their decisions. But is it a problem that most voters do not appear to be casting their ballots on the basis of candidates' views on issues? In an intraparty struggle is it reasonable to expect voters to use such cues because often contenders from the same party do not differ significantly in these matters? When assessing the criteria voters use, we need to consider the kinds of choices available to them.

Another concern about voters' decisions centers on the often large swings in support some candidates receive during primaries. These large shifts suggest that many voters are fickle and not well informed. Perhaps so, but national conventions have also experienced wild changes in support for candidates. In 1920, for instance, Warren G. Harding had little support during the first six ballots of the Republican convention. But by the tenth ballot, Harding became the GOP's presidential nominee. Does this rapid shift signify that party leaders are uninformed? Probably not, but the point is that we need to be careful when assessing the merits of voters' decisions.

Some scholars argue that the reliance on primaries has produced "media bosses."[5] The news media's coverage of the struggle for the nomination, these critics contend, results in swings in momentum for many contenders (Bartels 1988). Early victories provide extra news coverage for the winning candidate, generating votes, money, and campaign workers for subsequent primaries. This cycle feeds on itself and can, so the argument goes, catapult a candidate to the nomination. Of course, on the other side, candidates who do not do well in early contests can quickly drop from contention. But do the news media have too much influence on voters in primaries? Nelson Polsby (1983), for example, notes that voters in primaries are "overwhelmingly dependent for their information about politics on television and other forms of mass publicity . . ." (p. 76). Keech and Matthews (1976) suggest the media now perform the party's job of screening possible candidates for the nomination. These criticisms raise a number of questions. What exactly does "too much" influence mean? How does one know when the news media have the "right amount" of influence? Moreover, even if the news media have too much power, are they a bad source of information? Furthermore, can one eliminate the news media's effect on elections? The news media also affected the chances of candidates prior to the recent proliferation of primaries (David et al. 1960; Kelley 1962). Perhaps the news media would influence all nominating systems, not just the present arrangement.

A final criticism of relying on voters in primaries to select candidates is that they often choose contenders who lack broad support in the electorate (Polsby 1983). If voters tend to choose nominees that are only favored by narrow pluralities, then the likelihood of those candidates winning the general election is greatly reduced. In addition, such nominees may not be representative of the wishes of the party following, which has consequences not only for the election but also once these candidates assume office. There is some evidence for the claim that nominees often lack broad support—recall the ill-fated efforts of George McGovern and Walter Mondale. This criticism, however, may question the rules governing presidential primaries, not whether voters can select candidates with broad support. Under current rules, primaries provide poor estimates of voters' preferences for candidates, which may prevent the current system from picking the most popular candidate (and hence presumably the most electable). For instance, the rules that determine the allocation of delegates prevent an accurate measurement of popularity, since they can artificially make candidates appear more (or less) popular than they really are. Would changing the rules concerning the allocation of delegates increase the chances of nominating electable candidates? Primaries also only provide information about voters' first preferences. By relying solely on the first preferences of voters, nominees may not be supported by a majority of partisans. If we adopted a different ballot, would such problems end? These questions suggest that when assessing the characteristics of voters in primaries we also need to examine the rules, because the behavior of voters cannot be assessed without considering the environment in which they operate.

In general, the current nominating system is on the defensive. The perceived quality of recent nominees may be the real cause of much of this criticism. Critics have assessed the merits of contenders, such as Jimmy Carter and George McGovern, and concluded that a different system would probably have yielded better candidates. There are problems, however, with drawing conclusions on the basis of such evidence. First, since the proliferation of primaries, there have been ten nominations by the two major parties. In 1972 and 1984 the Republican incumbent was renominated without a struggle.[6] Therefore, voters in primaries have had to make a choice between potential nominees just eight times. With so few cases, conclusions about such a system must be made with care. Second, all systems can select bad presidents. While the current system selected Jimmy Carter—who is generally considered to have been a weak chief executive—previous systems also have selected uninspiring presidents such as James Buchanan, Ulysses Grant, Warren Harding, and Herbert Hoover. They stand in contrast to Ronald Reagan, who was able to work well with Congress and to keep a high rating in the Gallup Poll. The Reagan experience, however, seems to be ignored by many commentators on the current nominating system.

Critics of the present arrangement often seem to assume that a perfect system exists. In so doing they gloss over the fact that past systems have been criticized for many of the same reasons. The congressional caucus, for instance, was criticized for being unrepresentative of the party following.[7] Members of Congress were also criticized for the way they chose candidates.[8] The convention system faced similar attacks. Criticisms often focused on how party professionals selected nominees.[9] Woodrow Wilson (1911), for instance, questioned the quality of the convention's deliberations, because "[s]udden gusts of impulse are apt to change the whole feeling of the convention, and offset in a moment the most careful arrangements of managing politicians" (p. 62). Such unpredictability hardly instilled faith in the way party leaders attending those conventions chose candidates.[10] James Bryce (1891), for instance, contended that the convention system was one of the reasons "great men are not chosen president" (pp. 78–85). Attacks also centered on the representativeness of the national convention (Bryce 1891; Sait 1927; Ostrogorski 1921). The cumbersome nature of the convention system allowed party politicians the opportunity to control the selection process and hence choose a candidate of their own liking.[11]

The so-called mixed system also had its share of critics, resulting in a reform movement that transformed the nominating system.[12] This movement arose in part because critics felt the arrangement was not accurately representing the wishes of the rank and file but was instead representing the wishes of the party leadership. This complaint led McCarthy supporters to establish a commission on the delegate selection process headed by Governor Harold Hughes of Iowa (Shafer 1983). The Hughes

Commission report, *The Democratic Choice*, contended that the "mixed" system was too rigid to respond to "a relatively late-blooming but very strong wave of feeling among a large number of political activists when many delegate positions had already been filled at an earlier time, and when access to the rest of the delegate slots would be hard fought" (Polsby 1983, p. 28). These types of criticisms led to the formation of the McGovern-Frasier Commission. Its written report, *Mandate for Reform*, questioned the representativeness of the current system because all Democrats did not have a "full, meaningful, and timely opportunity to participate" in the selection of nominees (McGovern and Frasier 1970, p. 1). In short, critics questioned party leaders' control of the process and hence the quality of their decisions.

As one can see, there are common threads among the attacks made against all nominating systems. The validity of these complaints, however, is much less clear. Often calls for reform reflect partisan considerations. Progressives, such as Woodrow Wilson or Robert LaFollette, attacked party professionals because these progressives wanted a bigger role in the nomination of candidates and the party leaders were preventing it.[13] The McCarthyites' attacks on the mixed system also reflected the frustration that their candidate could not win the nomination. Even the current attacks made against the nominating system may reflect, in part, critics' preference for party leaders rather than voters in primaries to select candidates. We need, therefore, a systematic evaluation of presidential selectors to determine the accuracy of these complaints.

James Ceasar (1982) argues that the choice currently facing those who might change the nominating process is "whether to maintain the present system of direct democracy, with its limited role for political parties, or whether to transform the system into a representative decision-making process under the auspices of the political parties" (p. 179). This distinction does not describe completely the choice that faces politicians and legislators. The debate over how best to nominate candidates directly concerns the issue of whether voters in primaries or the party leadership should choose candidates. Or as Nelson Polsby and Aaron Wildavsky (1988) correctly ask: "Is the selection of presidential candidates best carried out by party leaders bargaining in conventions or by the mass electorate voting?" (p. 101).

This book shall provide a partial answer to this question. The answer will be partial because I am only addressing the common criticisms leveled against voters in primaries. I shall not be assessing the merits of party leaders to choose presidential candidates.[14] Nor will I be examining voters in caucuses. So even if voters in primaries are qualified to choose candidates, they still may be less qualified than party leaders or participants in caucuses. I shall leave those questions to others.

A LOOK AHEAD

At this point let me provide a brief look ahead. Chapter 2 deals with the issue of whether voters in primaries are representative of the party following. In these pages I propose an alternative conception of the party following based on the view that the party following should constitute a winning coalition in the general election. This new definition of the party following shows that voters in primaries are not more ideologically extreme than the party following. In fact, just the opposite is true, though for all practical matters the differences are politically insignificant. In Chapter 3 I tackle the issue of turnout in presidential primaries. Contrary to most previous research, I find that the amount of participation responds to the importance of the primary to the overall contest for the nomination. This finding suggests that the average rate of turnout is deceiving since a lot of contests are not important in selecting candidates. If one excludes those elections when calculating the average rate of turnout, participation is much higher than normally thought.

The next issue addressed in the book concerns how informed voters in primaries are (Chapter 4). Voters are clearly not as well informed as one would ideally like, especially in contests with three or more contenders. But when there are only two contenders, voters are about as well informed as voters in presidential elections. Problems emerge, however, when the number of candidates running is greater than three, which raises serious concerns about relying on voters to choose nominees. Chapter 5 examines how voters actually select candidates in presidential primaries. My findings suggest that voters pick contenders primarily based upon personal characteristics. While the news media supply much of the information voters rely upon, they still use substantive cues when selecting candidates. This criterion appears defensible, especially since candidates in primaries rarely offer clear choices on issues. But in the early contests when large numbers of candidates compete, voters appear to be unable to make good decisions.

The next chapter addresses the problem of the news media. Many critics of the current system cite the influence of the news media as one of the biggest weaknesses of the system. While there is no doubt that the media are important actors, Chapter 6 seeks to temper this claim. First, the media provide more substantive information about the candidates than generally thought, lessening concerns about the "horse-race" coverage. Second, while the actions of the news media affect the prospects of the contenders, this problem may not be as serious as many suggest—especially when one realizes that they were also important in shaping the chances of candidates in the previous nominating system.

Chapter 7 deals with how some of the rules governing presidential primaries may affect the behavior of voters in primaries; it will specifically address the concern that voters cannot select candidates with broad support in the electorate. This perceived weakness of voters, I contend, is due to the rules regulating the conduct of primaries. This chapter examines three different sets of rules and recommends changes in them to increase the chances that "electable" candidates are chosen.

The concluding chapter takes up the issue of reform. Using the findings of the six previous chapters, I develop a new presidential nominating system. The purpose of the reforms is to minimize the weaknesses of voters in primaries while taking advantage of their strengths. While the conclusions of the previous chapters find much merit in the many participants in primaries, there are still some important problems with relying on voters to choose candidates. Thus, if one seeks to maximize the chances that the nominating system will select good nominees, some changes must be made.

The arguments presented throughout this book will be based on a set of normative criteria. Some will object to these criteria and perhaps reasonably so. But the objective of all the arguments is to show that the question of the qualifications of voters in primaries is very much a value choice. Under some criteria they appear to be good decision-makers. Yet under another set of standards, one could easily call for the retrenchment of primaries and the reestablishment of the authority of party leaders. But since we are all motivated to some degree by partisan considerations, we need to be very sure of the accuracy of our claims before instituting another round of reforms. I hope the pages ahead move us in the right direction.

NOTES

1. Primaries existed prior to 1912, but these contests were not used for selecting delegates to the national conventions. See Louise Overacker (1926) and James Davis (1980) for useful histories of presidential primaries.

2. In the following races, the nominee also won the most votes in the primaries: the 1928, 1964, and 1968 Republican contests, and the 1912, 1928, 1932, 1956, and 1960 Democratic contests. The instances when the winner of the most votes did not capture the nominations were the 1912, 1916, 1920, 1936, 1940, 1944, and 1948 Republican races, and the 1920, 1924, 1952, and 1968 Democratic races. Most of the "competitive" races were contests where there were no incumbents running for renomination.

3. The only exception was George McGovern. But even in this case the outcome was very close. McGovern had only 68,000 fewer votes than Humphrey, about 0.5 percent.

4. I shall rely on other data as well. For instance, I have examined articles in newspapers and an array of videotapes of the paid advertising of the candidates and of the networks' coverage of the primaries.

In a recent study, Howard Reiter (1985) presents a lot of useful information about the nominating process. He correctly argues that all too often assertions are made about the system that are untested. While his work helps solve a number of important issues, he does not directly address the qualifications of voters in primaries.

5. Research relevant to this point includes Thomas Patterson (1980), David Weaver et al. (1981), and Polsby (1983).

6. This statement is not entirely accurate, since Nixon did face opposition from Paul McCloskey and John Ashbrook in 1972. But neither challenger mounted a serious effort.

7. See M. Ostrogorski (1900, 1921), C. S. Thompson (1902), James Chase (1973), William Carleton (1953) and Austin Ranney (1975). There were two reasons given for why members of Congress were thought to be unrepresentative of the party following. First, as Carleton (1953) notes, "Federalists who lived in districts represented in Congress by Republicans, and Republicans who lived in districts represented by Federalists or nonparty members were not represented in [the] presidential nominating [process] . . ." (p. 147). In later years, in an attempt to correct this problem, additional representatives from the districts attended the caucuses, but this adjustment did not deflect much of the criticism. See Ostrogorski (1921) for a more detailed discussion (p. 14). Second, since there was generally only one candidate from each party on the ballot in a general election, voters could not have chosen between factions of the party.

8. Thompson (1902) and Ostrogorski (1921) make this criticism. It generally involved the fact that the negotiations involved in selecting candidates were closed to the public. In 1800, for example, Jefferson was the obvious choice for the Republican nomination, but the vice-presidential candidate was a question mark. The same problem existed for the Federalists: Adams was the choice for president, but the nominee for vice-president remained unclear. In both caucuses, bargaining took place concerning these positions and the secret negotiations generated criticism of the caucus. Thompson (1902), in writing about the 1800 caucuses, argued that "secret machinations of this character were not likely to decrease the unfavorable criticism which the Caucus at once met. For in spite of their long familiarity with the system in its undeveloped form, the minds of many people were becoming strongly prejudiced against it . . ." (pp. 22–25). With secret negotiations, Congress could be more easily corrupted than in an open forum of nomination. In an attempt to mute some of the charges of corruption, the caucus went public in 1804.

9. James Bryce (1891), for instance, argued that the convention fell "under the control of selfish intriguers and [destroyed] the chances of able and independent men . . ." (p. 172). Edward Sait (1927) described the membership of a Cook County convention in 1896 that elected delegates to the national convention: "Among the 723 delegates 17 had been tried for homicide, 46 had served terms in the penitentiary for homicide or other felonies, 84 were identified by detectives as having criminal records" (p. 269). These kinds of credentials question the motives of politicians and hence the criteria used by the delegates when selecting nominees. Ernest Meyers (1902) concurred with Sait, arguing that conventions present "an almost ideal soil for intrigue and corruption" (p. 22). He also called conventions a "profitable business" (p. 26).

10. See Donald Collat, Stanley Kelley, and Ronald Rogowski (1981) for a useful discussion of bandwagons in national conventions. They analyze the often large swings in support for candidates at the convention and suggest that "something other than assessments of candidates' merits guides the voting of many delegates" (p. 426).

11. Of course, one could argue that the party leaders' desire to gain office gave them incentive to represent the party following, otherwise they would risk losing the general election (Schattschneider 1942).

12. For a detailed account of this election and the time following, see Byron Shafer (1983).

13. Ranney (1975) carefully develops a similar line of argument when explaining the changes in the nominating system.

14. There have been some recent studies of convention delegates that provide insight into the characteristics of these actors. See Warren Miller and M. Kent Jennings (1986) and Miller (1988) for two insightful analyses of delegates to the national party conventions. For an interesting study of delegates to state party conventions see Alan Abramowitz and Walter Stone (1984).

2

The Representativeness of Voters in Presidential Primaries

One of the most common and troubling criticisms of voters in primaries is that they are unrepresentative of the party following. V. O. Key (1956) was probably the first to voice this concern about participants in primaries, arguing that "the effective primary constituency . . . may come to consist predominantly of the people of certain sections of a state, or persons of specific national origin or religious affiliation, of people especially responsive to certain styles of political leadership or shades of ideology, or of groups markedly unrepresentative in one way or another of the party following" (p. 153). While Key presented some aggregate data to support his suspicions, subsequent scholars have contended that voters who participate in the 30 or so presidential primaries are better educated, better paid, and more ideologically extreme than the party following (Ranney 1972; Ladd 1978; Lengle 1981; Polsby 1983; Keeter and Zukin 1983; Crotty and Jackson 1985).

If these critics are correct, serious questions arise about relying on voters in primaries to choose presidential nominees. If voters in primaries, for instance, are more ideologically extreme in their orientation to politics than the party following, the candidates chosen by voters may reflect this ideological bias (Lengle 1981). Such nominees could have difficult time winning general elections since they would have limited success in appealing to the moderate voters who are essential to a victory in November. Given that a major objective of any political party to win elections, these kinds of outcomes would be troublesome. A further implication of these claims is that if ideologically extreme elements of each party dominate the nominating process, parties in general may not be responsive to the electorate at large. As Everett Ladd (1978) a gues, the recent "party reforms serve the interests of the upper middle class" (p. 59). This concern has serious ramifications for whether our political system can meet the needs of the entire public since it questions the very foundation of our democratic system.

Whether voters in primaries are representative of each party's following, however, is not a question easily answered. To answer it, one must first decide who should be represented. That is, who is or should be the "party following"? Ranney (1975) once observed that "just about every conflict over making the parties more representative . . . turns on the basic question of who should be treated as party members" (p. 145). As the initial chapter indicates, all previous systems of presidential nominations have been criticized for being "unrepresentative." And most of these complaints were generated by competing ideas of who should be represented by the system. For instance, the congressional caucus was attacked by state and local party leaders, in part, because it was members of Congress, not these local politicians, who were receiving representation. Consequently, one must consider a variety of possible definitions of the "party following" and decide which is the most desirable. Once this task is accomplished, then one can begin to determine if indeed voters in primaries are unrepresentative of the party following.

A DEFINITION OF THE "PARTY FOLLOWING"

Previous studies have used a variety of different conceptions of the party following. Comparisons have been drawn between voters in primaries and those who did not vote in the primaries (Ranney and Epstein 1966; Ranney 1968 and 1972), voters in primaries and party identifiers (Kritzer 1977; Lengle 1981), voters in primaries and voters in the general election who failed to vote in the primaries (Norrander 1989) and voters in primaries and all voters in general elections (DiNitto and Smithers 1972; Kritzer 1977; Rubin 1980). Most of these comparisons, however, are inadequate because they often include people who may or may not be supporters of the party. Any good definition of the party following should constitute those individuals who are likely to turn out and are likely to support the party in the November election. Otherwise, the party risks representing those individuals who have no intention of voting for the party in the general election. Most studies, however, have made little effort to identify the "followers" of either party. Comparisons, for instance, between all voters in primaries and all voters in general elections have limited value since supporters of both parties are lumped together. James Lengle (1981), on the other hand, criticizes the use of only nonvoters as the base of comparison:

The important empirical question, as originally posed by Key, is whether the primary electorate consists of groups markedly unrepresentative of the party following. The answer is found, not by comparing two mutually exclusive parts, that is, primary voters with non-voters, but by comparing the part with the whole, that is, the primary electorate (voters) with the *entire party membership* [my emphasis]. (pp. 11–12)

His argument is important because it points to the fact that non-voters may not be members of the party.

On the basis of this reasoning Lengle uses party identification as a proxy for the party following. Though his approach is superior to most other efforts, there are still problems with this conception of the party following. One should, for instance, expect voters in primaries to be unrepresentative of the party identifiers since the latter group includes large numbers of habitual nonvoters. Nonvoters, of course, tend to be from lower socioeconomic groups than voters. Consequently, by including these nonvoters in the "party following," one would automatically increase the proportion of the less well-off. This increase would, in turn, affect the ideological composition of the party following since the less well-off tend to be less ideologically extreme than the better-off. So the findings of Lengle and others that primary electorates are more ideologically extreme than the "party following" may, in part, be a result of the definition used.[1]

There is another, more important, problem in using party identifiers as a proxy for the party following: it provides a poor idea about those who generally support the party in the general election. Votes in the general election, not identification with a party, are the important issue for parties when trying to win general elections. The leaders of the parties want to represent, and hence consider, the views of a potentially *winning* coalition in the general election. And since neither party constitutes a majority of the electorate, as measured by self-identification, the party leadership needs to consider the views of other potential party voters when choosing a candidate. In short, by using party identifiers previous studies have not examined directly the behavior that is central to a party's effort to win in November.

A good proxy, then, for the followers of a party can be found in those who vote in general elections. Specifically, the following should be made up of those who usually vote for the party's candidates, those who lean toward the party yet do not always vote for its candidates, and those independents and opposing partisans who occasionally support the party in the general election. This line of argument has long been recognized by political scientists. As Key (1964) once argued, if a party is to win the general election, it "must maintain the loyalty of its own standpatters; it must also concern itself with the great block of voters uncommitted to either party as well as those who may be weaned away from the opposition" (p. 220). Given these guidelines for a successful coalition, a good proxy for the party following would be general-election voters who identify with the party and those who voted for the party yet do not identify with the party. The party following, therefore, consists of two parts. The first part is all identifiers of the party who turned out, regardless of whom they voted for. While this group includes some individuals who "defected" from the party, presumably their self-identification indicates a general tendency to support the party in the general election. To use Key's word, this group is the "standpatters." The second component of the party following is independents and members of the opposition who supported the party in that general election. These people are the "occasional" party supporters.

This definition has a number of advantages. First, the party following consists of a potential winning coalition in the general election.[2] This aspect of the definition is very attractive since it gets at the central concern of most politicians: winning elections. A second, and somewhat related, advantage of the definition is that independents and wavering partisans of the other party who support the party in that general election are included among the party followers. Struggles over these voters are where elections are won and lost. A third advantage is that by comparing two sets of voters I avoid the built-in bias that exists when including nonvoters in one's definition of the party following.

Underlying these "pragmatic" reasons for adopting this definition is a normative ideal: parties should seek to represent those people who are likely to turn out and support the party in the general election. It strikes me as perverse to represent those who do not support the party in the general election either because they do not vote at all or vote for the opposing party. Yet this is exactly what occurs under the definitions used by other scholars. This outcome is ironic since many political scientists who advocated alternative proxies for the party following probably did in fact want to represent those who vote for the party in the general election.

Although this definition may have some appeal, there are some drawbacks to it. In deciding whether voters in primaries are representative of the party following, I shall be able only to examine the demographic characteristics and ideological composition of both groups. I cannot assess voters' and followers' attitudes on issues or preferences for candidates. The campaign differs in primaries and general elections, preventing any meaningful comparison. In 1980, for example, 55.6 percent of voters in Democratic primaries favored some increase in defense spending. Among Democratic voters in the general election, the proportion jumped to 76.5 percent. Was this increase the result of Reagan's call for a military buildup in the general election or because the two electorates differed on that issue? One cannot tell.[3] The same problem exists for assessing the electorate's preferences for candidates since preferences measured during the heat of a primary may well change by the time the general election rolls around.[4]

Inability to compare preferences for candidates poses perhaps the most serious problem for my definition because agreement between voters and party followers in preferences for candidates is probably the most important consideration in assessing the representativeness of a nominating system.[5] Yet even if one uses self-identification as a proxy for the party following, there is a potential problem with using preferences for candidates to assess the representativeness of voters in presidential primaries. At the outset of most contested campaigns for the presidential nomination, a large proportion of the electorate either has weak preferences or no preference at all, making these preferences highly volatile.[6] Consequently, the results of each contest greatly influence the preferences of voters and party identifiers. As Bartels (1985, 1988) and others have shown, "momentum" shapes voters' preferences. Thus, one should *expect* there to be some convergence in attitudes between voters in primaries and self-identified partisans as the campaign progresses. Results from the 1980 NES Panel Study lend support to this idea. By June 1980, there was general agreement between voters in primaries and party identifiers.[7] This agreement, however, is not clear evidence of the representativeness of voters in primaries; it may simply demonstrate the influence of the campaign on voters' and partisans' preferences for candidates. In short, an accurate reading of preferential representation is exceedingly difficult to obtain because of the confounding effects from the sequence of presidential primaries.

Nonetheless, by focusing only on the demographic characteristics and the ideological composition of voters in primaries and their respective party following I shall still be able to address the question of representativeness. First, much of the criticism leveled against primary voters centers on their demographic and ideological composition (Lengle 1981). Second, it is likely that demographic characteristics and ideological positions are related to preferences for candidates. A "liberal" voter, for instance, was more likely to favor Senator Kennedy over President Carter in 1980 or Governor Dukakis over Senator Gore in 1988.

DATA

In assessing the representativeness of voters in primaries, I shall use data from CBS/*New York Times* and ABC/*Washington Post* exit polls in 1976, 1980, and 1984. I shall be able to examine 18 Democratic primaries and 5 Republican primaries.[8] These data should serve my purposes very well since exit polls provide reliable estimates of who voted in primaries and in general elections (Levy 1983).[9]

There is another important advantage of these data. Previous studies generally have examined only one or two elections (Ranney 1968, 1972; Lengle 1981). Yet a single election may have certain features that encourage unrepresentativeness. If a black (such as Jesse Jackson) runs in a primary, blacks may be more likely to vote. If blacks turn out at a higher rate than normal, the results could suggest overrepresentation or mask underrepresentation that occurs for blacks in the absence of such a candidacy. Specific issues in the campaign may also promote unrepresentativeness in a given election. If an issue, such as gun control or abortion, is very salient to a particular group, its members may turn out at a higher rate than normal. It is important, therefore, to base an accurate test of representativeness on a wide range of cases so as to avoid the idiosyncratic factors associated with any one race. Fortunately, I have a number of data points to study this problem—a luxury most previous studies have not enjoyed.

THE RESULTS

Tables 2.1 and 2.2 present the demographic differences between voters in primaries and party followers.[10] In stark contrast to the findings of previous works, the Democratic following is *better* educated and *better* paid than voters in Democratic primaries.[11] While this pattern was not completely consistent, the differences were generally sizable. On average, the party following were 8 percentage points more likely to have college educations than were voters in 1976 and 1980 Democratic primaries. In 1984 the figure was even higher. A similar pattern exists for differences in income between the two groups. For instance, in New York (1980) about 70 percent of the Democratic following earned at least $15,000, while only about 57 percent of primary voters had a similar income.

Comparable trends emerge in the Republican camp. The voters in Republican primaries were generally less well-paid and had less formal education than their party following. Among the college educated, there was more than a 4 percentage point gap between voters in Republican primaries and their followers. Although the gap in education among the Democrats was larger, there still could be sizable differences. In Illinois (1980), for instance, 47 percent of the Republican following had completed college compared to about 35 percent of voters in primaries.

Another consistent difference between voters in primaries and the following of both parties is that the former are older than the latter. On average, voters in Democratic primaries overrepresented the 60-and-over age group by 8 percentage points in 1976 and 1980, and by about 6 percentage points in 1984. Among Republicans the comparable difference was 10 percentage points. In California (1980), for instance, about 26 percent of voters in Democratic primaries were over 60 years old, while

Table 2.1

The Difference Between Voters in Presidential Primaries and the "Party Following," 1976 and 1980

	Democrats		Republicans	
	Mean Difference+	Times Consistent$	Mean Difference+	Times Consistent$
Sex				
Female	-.4	50.0	-2.9	80.0
Race				
Black	2.0	70.0	.7	50.0
White	-3.1	70.0	-.2	50.0
Age				
18-29	-8.0	100	-4.6	80.0
30-59	-.3	43.0	-5.7	80.0
60+	8.3	83.0	10.3	100
Education				
> High School	6.6	100	1.2	50.0
High School	2.7	80.0	1.1	50.0
> College	-1.3	60.0	2.2	75.0
College	-8.2	100	-4.4	75.0
Religion				
Protestant	-2.7	50.0	10.4	100
Catholic	-3.0	43.0	-9.2	100
Income&				
Low	3.8	70.0	2.4	67.0
Middle	1.5	70.0	1.9	80.0
High	-5.3	80.0	-4.3	80.0
Union Member				
Yes	2.1	67.0	-3.8	60.0
Number of Cases	7		5	

+The "mean difference" is the average difference between the proportion of voters and followers in a given demographic category across the various samples. A negative value indicates that these electorates underrepresent the party following.

$The proportion of "times consistent" indicates whether all samples agreed with the general pattern of representation for that particular category. A value of 67, for example, means that one-third of the surveys disagree with the direction of the "mean difference."

&Income was coded differently in 1976 and 1980. In 1980 the "high" group earned over $15,000, while in 1976 that figure was $12,000. I have treated these two categories as the same. These figures may not seem to be "high" income, but due to differences in coding this was the only breakdown that was possible without throwing away cases. The "middle" figure is $8,000 to $12,000 in 1976 and $10,000 to $15,000 in 1980. The "low" figure is below $8,000 in 1976 and below $10,000 in 1980.
Source: CBS/New York Times and ABC/Washington Post exit polls.

Table 2.2
**The Difference Between Voters in Presidential Primaries and the
"Party Following," 1984**

| | Democrats | |
	Mean Difference	Times Consistent
Sex		
Female	-1.4	77.0
Race		
Black	1.0	67.0
White	-1.1	67.0
Age		
18-29	-5.3	100
30-44	-2.9	100
45-59	2.4	89.0
60+	5.8	100
Education		
College	-12.8	100
Income		
Below $12,500	1.7	67.0
12,500-25,000	-.2	55.0
25,000-35,000	.6	60.0
35,000-50,000	-.1	57.0
Above $50,000	-1.9	70.0
Union Member		
Yes	.1	50.0
Number of Cases	11	

*For descriptions of the numbers in this table, see
Table 2.1.

Source: CBS/New York Times exit polls.

among the party following the figure was only 15 percent. On the Republican side, 15 percent of voters in Ohio's primary were under 29 years old, while 23 percent of the Republican following fell in this age group.

When examining other demographic categories, such as race, sex, and union membership, there were few consistent differences between voters and followers of both parties.[12] Blacks, for instance, seem to be slightly overrepresented among voters in Democratic primaries. Women, on the other hand, appear to be well represented in Democratic primaries but slightly underrepresented in Republican primaries. In neither party were the differences in union membership consistent, suggesting that misrepresentation is not a problem. In general, the differences in these categories tend to be small and inconsistent.

Table 2.3 reports the ideological affiliations of voters in primaries and party followers. As one can see, Democratic followers are *more* liberal than voters in Democratic primaries in five of the six cases studied. In Pennsylvania (1980), for instance, 32 percent of the Democratic follow-

Table 2.3
The Difference in the Ideological Composition of Voters in Presidential Primaries and the "Party Following"

	Democrats		Republicans	
	Mean Difference	Times Consistent	Mean Difference	Times Consistent
Liberal&	-4.5	85.0	-2.5	75.0
Moderate	3.2	67.0	4.1	75.0
Conservative	1.3	67.0	-2.6	75.0
Sample Size	18		5	

*For a description of numbers in this table, see Table 2.1.

&In each of these surveys the liberal-conservative question was coded and worded the same. The question lacked a "don't know" category, however. The absence of such a category greatly inflates the proportion of "ideological" respondents since those respondents who do not think in liberal-conservative terms could not say so. This omission should not, however, pose a problem, since my objective is to compare the two groups, not assess how ideological a particular electorate is.

Source: CBS/New York Times and ABC/Washington Post exit polls.

ing labeled themselves liberal while only 22 percent of voters in Democratic primaries did so. On the Republican side of the ledger, the differences were about the same, as it appears that voters in primaries are slightly more moderate than the party followers. Of the five cases, only voters in California's 1980 Republican primary were more conservative than the party following.

AN EXPLANATION

The results in Tables 2.1, 2.2, and 2.3 show that voters in primaries are less educated, less well-paid, and more moderate in their ideological views than the party following—results that run directly counter to the conventional wisdom on the subject. In explaining these findings, skeptics, of course, might point to the proxy I am using for the party following. I did test other definitions of the party following, but the results remained the same.[13] Certainly, comparing voters in primaries to a subset of those who vote in general elections accounts for some of the differences between voters and followers. Nonetheless, these critics would still not expect this particular party following to be better educated, better paid, and more ideologically extreme than voters in primaries. The accepted view of scholars is that "low stimulus" primary elections would tend to attract voters who are more ideologically extreme and generally better off than those in the "high stimulus" general election. The explanation for these findings may lie in the relationship between age and turnout in primaries and general elections.

As Tables 2.1 and 2.2 demonstrated, older voters make up a larger proportion of primary electorates than of the party following. These older voters tend to have less education, less income, and a more moderate orientation to politics, which may account for much of the differences between voters and followers. For instance, while having a high school education is now commonplace among younger citizens, it was uncommon for those who are currently over 60 years old to have completed 12 years of school. Even among those who turned out in Pennsylvania's Democratic primary (1980), 46 percent of those participants over 60 years old had less than a high school education, while only 3 percent of the 18 to 29 year olds had not completed high school. This pattern is similar for all the states studied. With less education, these citizens probably did not make as much money as they would have made with a better education. Moreover, a good proportion of this group are retired and probably live on fixed incomes. Such individuals will tend to have lower incomes than those who are still working 9-to-5 jobs. Consequently, it should be no surprise that in Ohio's Republican primary (1980) about 26 percent of those over 60 earned less than $10,000, while only 18 percent of those between the ages of 18 and 29 had a similar income. Since older voters are generally not as well off or as well educated as other elements of the electorate, they will tend to be more moderate in their ideological orientation to politics. In short, these demographic differences between the young and the old coupled with the fact that the 60-and-over cohort constitutes a higher proportion of the electorate in primaries than in general elections probably explain much of the differences found in the above tables.

The reasons why older voters turn out in disproportionate numbers, I suspect, is that older voters tend to be more partisan than younger ones. For instance, results from the 1980 National Election Study show that only about 8 percent of those citizens over 60 were self-identified independents, while about 19 percent of those citizens under 29 labeled themselves independent. In the 1984 presidential election, Herbert Asher (1988) reports that among citizens between 55 and 70, 40 percent were "strong" partisans. In contrast, only 22 percent of citizens between 21 and 30 viewed themselves as ardent supporters of a party. As one might expect, partisans tend to be more interested in the prenomination campaign than independents.[14] With greater interest, partisans will be more likely to participate in primaries, accounting for the high rate of turnout among this oldest cohort.[15] In addition, some states require that an individual register as a member of that party in order to participate—

something that a partisan is more likely to do. Thus, legal barriers help prevent the less partisan from voting. In short, a consequence of the dwindling partisanship among younger voters may be that older, more partisan voters have a disproportionate influence in primaries.

A useful way to think about why older voters turn out in greater numbers in primaries is to borrow Angus Campbell's (1960) famous distinction between "core" and "peripheral" voters. "Core" voters consist "of people whose level of political interest is sufficiently high to take them to the polls in all national elections, even those in which the level of political stimulation is relatively weak" (p. 399). "Peripheral" voters, on the other hand, are those voters "whose level of political interest is lower but whose motivation to vote has been sufficiently increased by the stimulation of the election situation to carry them to the polls" (p. 399). Since presidential primaries are "low stimulus" events in comparison with presidential elections, the former should have a higher proportion of "core" voters than the latter. In most elections, "interest" is strongly related to socioeconomic status—the better off tend to be more interested in the campaign than the less well-off (Verba and Nie 1972). In a partisan affair such as a primary, "interest" is also a function of one's partisanship. Consequently, the "core" does participate in large numbers in primaries as Campbell's theory would suggest, but this "core" is made up of the less well-off, but more partisan, elements of society.

IMPLICATIONS AND CONCLUSION

It turns out that Key's original argument is correct—voters in primaries are unrepresentative of the party following. Key (1956) himself was unsure of how this unrepresentativeness would influence outcomes, arguing that "the exact form of these consequences would . . . be a product of the facts of the situation as they existed in a particular state at a particular time" (p. 153). The belief that voters in primaries are better paid, better educated, and more ideologically extreme than the party following came from scholars who sought to test Key's idea. By failing to consider alternative definitions of the "party following" and by not having access to a variety of cases, they drew misleading conclusions. Of course, one could contend that my results are problematic because my definition of the party following is suspect. Such an argument might have merit, especially if one does not believe that the major purpose of parties is to win elections and, therefore, the "party following" should not consist of a potentially winning coalition. But many of these scholars share the belief that parties should strive to win elections, suggesting that my definition should have much appeal to them (Lengle 1981, p. 9; Polsby 1983, pp. 85–88).

Even though I have raised doubts about previous work in this area, voters in primaries are still unrepresentative of the party following. The consequences of this unrepresentativeness, however, are less severe for parties than they would be if voters in primaries were more ideologically extreme. The chances that parties cater to ideologically extreme elements because of primaries appear slim, since voters in primaries are more moderate in their orientation to politics than previously thought. This change suggests that primaries do not undermine the responsiveness of parties to the more moderate elements of the rank and file. Actually, just the reverse appears to be true. That is, voters in primaries show a slight bias toward the more moderate wing of the party following.

The more immediate implication of these findings involves the parties' chances for victory in November. When scholars believed that voters in primaries were more ideologically extreme than the party following, there was concern that the nominees might reflect this bias and hence be less "electable." But my evidence suggests that voters in primaries are more moderate than the party following, which should ease such concerns. In fact, if general elections are a struggle for the "middle" of the ideological spectrum, the presidential primary may be especially able to produce nominees capable of competing successfully in them.

While there have been only a handful of candidates nominated under the current system, one can crudely test to see if the system tends to produce "moderate" or "extreme" nominees. George McGovern would certainly be labeled as a "noncentrist" by most observers, but the other nominees have tended to be "moderate." In fact, moderate candidates have often defeated more "extreme" challengers for the nomination— Carter in 1976 and 1980, Ford in 1976, Mondale in 1984,[16] Bush in 1988, and Dukakis in 1988. One might point to Reagan as an "ideologically extreme" nominee, but he did go on to victory in November, suggesting that he was not so "extreme" as to alienate over 50 percent of the voters. In short, while the evidence is not overwhelming, the nominees selected under this arrangement have tended to be somewhat moderate in their orientation to politics—a finding that is consistent with the results presented in this chapter.

Actually, the kinds of differences reported in Tables 2.1, 2.2, and 2.3 are unlikely to have much effect on who is nominated. For instance, even if one assumes that moderates are overrepresented by 15 percent in primary electorates (almost five times the amount actually shown in Table 2.3 for the Democrats and four times for Republicans) and one further assumes that moderates differ in their preferences from liberals by 25 percentage points (an unusually large difference according to my data), the effect on the share of the two-candidate vote is less than 2 percentage points.[17] In a three-candidate race with only one moderate contender, the potential bias is only about 3 percentage points.[18] The only time such biases might make a difference would be in very close elections. Yet even in close elections the effect will generally be modest since many states use some form of proportional representation to allocate delegates in presidential primaries. If delegates were distributed, however, on a "winner-take-all" basis, then there might be more cause for concern since in a close race such a bias might tip the scales to one of the candidates. But even so, this kind of bias is not a major concern when trying to pick an "electable" candidate since a moderate contender generally would have more success in November than more "extreme" challengers. Actually, the amount of bias may decline even further in the future as generational replacement reduces the differences in partisanship among the old and the young.[19]

The most important implication of the findings in this chapter involves our assessment of voters in primaries. As indicated in the introduction to this study, voters in primaries are under attack by many leading scholars of political parties (Ranney 1975; Ceasar 1979, 1982; Polsby 1983). A major reason for their unfavorable assessments is the belief that they were more ideologically extreme than the party following. The evidence presented here should ease these concerns. Or at the very least, scholars should consider other features of the system that may be fostering these perceived weaknesses. Of course, any changes in assessment would still depend on one's answer to the question raised at the outset: Who should be represented in the nominating system? But if one believes that the system should represent those most likely to bring the party a victory in November, then perhaps we should be less critical of voters in primaries.

Of course, this finding is only one piece of the puzzle concerning the qualifications of voters in primaries. There are still other complaints lodged against voters, which we shall address in future chapters.

NOTES

1. As evidence of how Lengle's definition may create artificial bias, I compared voters in general elections to all party identifiers. As I expected, voters tended to be better educated and better paid than party identifiers. For instance, 20 percent of voters had less than a high school education, while 25 percent of identifiers failed to complete high school. The 5 percentage point gap supports my contention that party identifiers include a number of nonvoters, which lowers the socioeconomic standing of the whole group.

2. In almost every case examined later, the party following constituted over 50 percent of those who voted in the general election. The only exception was New Hampshire in 1984. It is difficult to forge a winning Democratic coalition given this state's strong Republican leanings. This kind of incident, however, is quite uncommon.

3. Actually, a panel study would be able to answer this question, but the data I use are not from that kind of survey.

4. To complicate matters further, as the election year progresses, the electorate becomes better informed (Patterson 1980). This additional information results in a decrease in "don't know" responses, which may affect the distribution of opinion on these matters and also may lead to changes in position on them.

5. Lengle (1981), for example, states: "A strong argument could be made that demographic unrepresentativeness, its severity and pervasiveness notwithstanding, is irrelevant as long as ideology, issue concerns, and *more importantly*, candidate preferences are unrelated to, or independent of, the socio-economic status of Democrats" (p. 25, my emphasis).

6. For instance, among Democratic party identifiers in Erie, Pennsylvania (1976), 27 percent did not have a preference for any of the contenders for their party's nomination. For Republicans in Erie, over 30 percent of identifiers responded "don't know" to the question about preferences. The rapid rise of contenders such as Gary Hart, George Bush, and Jimmy Carter points in the same direction. Chapter 5 provides a good deal of evidence that indicates that many citizens have weakly held preferences.

7. Specifically, about 61 percent of Democratic primary voters preferred Carter while over 58 percent of Democratic identifiers supported the incumbent president for renomination. On the Republican side, 54 percent of the primary voters cast ballots for Reagan and 55 percent of Republican identifiers supported the former governor.

8. The Republican primaries were held in the following states: California (1976, 1980), Pennsylvania (1980), Illinois (1980), and Ohio (1980). On the Democratic side, the states were New York (1976, 1980, 1984), California (1976, 1980, 1984), Pennsylvania (1980, 1984), Illinois (1980, 1984), Ohio (1980, 1984), New Hampshire (1984), Massachusetts (1984), Alabama (1984), Georgia (1984), Oregon (1984), and Indiana (1984).

9. By surveying only voters, exit polls avoid the overestimation of turnout that plagues surveys relying on self-reported votes. David Moore and Richard Hofstetter (1973) argue, for instance, that 30 percent of those who claimed to have voted did not. James DeNardo (1988) lends additional support to this point, arguing that "self-reported rates of turnout in the SRC/CPS surveys consistently exceed official figures by 13 to 20 percentage points," suggesting that even carefully conducted surveys may "provide a distorted picture of the actual voting electorates" (p. 15).

10. I have presented two tables because there were numerous coding differences in 1984, making it extremely difficult to merge data from 1976 and 1980 with that of 1984.

11. These results contradict the findings of the Winograd commission. This Democratic party commission found that voters in primaries were better educated and better paid than Democratic voters in general elections (Winograd 1978, pp. 11–13). My data support the opposite conclusion. What accounts for these differences? First, the Winograd study uses only Democratic voters rather than Democratic voters and identifiers as I have. When I excluded party identifiers from my data, however, the results still contradict those in the Winograd study. The answer may lie in how the Winograd commission defined Democratic

voters. They based their estimates on samples of *likely* voters. Relying on such data may greatly inflate the number of respondents who are treated as voters. Exit polls, on the other hand, survey only voters.

12. There is one other consistent difference. Republican followers are much more likely to be Catholic than are voters in Republican primaries. This difference is probably attributable to the number of Catholics who "defect" to the Republican party in general elections.

13. One alternative conception included only those respondents who were both Democratic voters *and* identifiers as a proxy for the Democratic following. Another possible way to define the party following is to use all voters in the general election who identify with the party, regardless of how they voted in the general election. In both cases, however, the data point to similar conclusions—voters in primaries are not from higher socioeconomic groups than these other "followings."

14. In January 1980, 30 percent of independents were "not very interested" in the campaign. This figure stands in contrast to only 19 percent of Democratic identifiers and 15 percent of Republican identifiers who were "not much interested" in the campaign.

15. Data from the 1980 CPS National Election Study further confirm that older voters are more likely to turn out in primaries than in general elections when compared to the younger cohort. Specifically the data indicate that the 60-and-over age group has a two-and-a-half-times greater participation rate in primaries than the 18-to-29 cohort, while in the general election this figure declines to less than one and a half times.

16. Mondale's nomination does not really fit in with the other cases mentioned since he and his main challenger, Gary Hart, were very close on the so-called ideological spectrum. Mondale (and Hart) did, however, fend off liberal challenges by Alan Cranston, Jesse Jackson, and George McGovern.

17. I arrive at this figure as follows: Assume a two-candidate race in which moderates prefer one candidate to the other by 75 percent to 25 percent, liberals split their vote 50–50 between the two candidates, and conservatives split 80 percent to 20 percent in their preferences. In addition, the moderates constitute 50 percent of the following and 65 percent of the voters. The rest of the electorate in both cases is split evenly among liberals and conservatives.

Even in Lengle's (1981) study of California's 1972 Democratic primary, he found only a bias of 3 to 5 percentage points in McGovern's share of the vote attributable to the "unrepresentativeness" he uncovered. Given his approach to the problem, his findings may be in error. But in any case, the magnitude of the bias is small, pointing to the fact that even when there appears to be much unrepresentativeness the effects are rarely very large.

As a side note, California was a very unusual case. Not only was California the last primary in a hotly contested nomination, but the winner, McGovern, received all the delegates in this large state because of the "winner-take-all" rule. The combination of these factors exaggerated the effect of this perceived bias that Lengle reports.

18. I have made a number of assumptions to arrive at this figure. First, there are three candidates in the race—one liberal, one moderate, and one conservative. The "liberal" vote is divided among the contenders as follows: the liberal

candidate receives 50 percent, the moderate candidate 30 percent, and the conservative candidate 20 percent. The "moderate" vote is divided in a similar fashion: the liberal candidate receives 30 percent, the moderate candidate 50 percent, and the conservative candidate 20 percent. The "conservative" vote is split in the following manner: the liberal candidate receives 20 percent, the moderate candidate 30 percent, and the conservative candidate 50 percent. The final set of assumptions concerns the makeup of the electorate. I assumed the following distribution in the electorate:

	Voters	**"Followers"**
Liberals	25 %	30 %
Moderates	50 %	40 %
Conservatives	25 %	30 %

As one can see, the moderates are overrepresented by 10 percent. Of course, one could adjust these assumptions and uncover different "biases," but the point is that there is not much effect on the outcome of presidential primaries.

19. If a realignment took place, a new "core" might emerge, changing radically who votes in primaries. Such a change could also alter many of my findings.

═ 3 ═

Participation in Presidential Primaries

Another frequently heard criticism of voters in primaries is that too few of them participate in presidential primaries. Davis (1980) observes that "voter turnout in key presidential primaries remains disappointingly low— less than 30 percent of the voting age population (VAP)—despite celebrity level coverage by television networks and the national press" (p. 134). Ceasar (1982) concurs, commenting that "voter turnout in primaries is rather low . . ." (p. 65). While the rate of participation is far from ideal, it is not clear that turnout in primaries has been "disappointingly low" or "rather low." For instance, if one seeks to maximize grass-roots participation in the choice of presidential nominees, a defensible goal, then primaries are a clear success. Alternative methods for selecting delegates generally have lower rates of participation. Citizens, for instance, turn out in much larger numbers in primaries than in caucuses. As many as 18 times more participants turn out in primaries than in caucuses. On average, primaries "draw roughly one-half of a party's eligible electorate, whereas caucuses tend to draw about one-twentieth" (Crotty and Jackson 1985, p. 84).

Of course, many of those who complain of low turnout in primaries are comparing it to rates in general elections, not to participation in caucuses. Ranney (1977) contends that "while turnout in presidential elections may be a respectable stream (if not a mighty river), turnout in presidential primaries is a small brook" (p. 26). That turnout in primaries is lower than in general elections is not an obvious reason for concern since the costs of voting in primaries are greater than in general elections. First, less information is available about all the candidates during primaries than in general elections, increasing the cost of acquiring it.

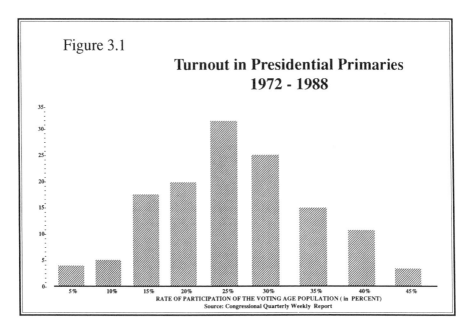

Figure 3.1

Turnout in Presidential Primaries
1972 - 1988

RATE OF PARTICIPATION OF THE VOTING AGE POPULATION (in PERCENT)
Source: Congressional Quarterly Weekly Report

For instance, candidates often spend little time campaigning in primaries, making information scarce. By comparison, the voters in general elections have had the benefit of over nine months of campaigning.[1] Second, while partisanship cuts the cost of acquiring information in general elections, it does little to ease costs when choosing candidates in primaries. Third, the direct primary is a more complicated electoral device than the general election. The vote in a primary does not go directly to the candidate but rather to convention delegates who are usually bound to that candidate. Such procedures may serve to confuse citizens and add to their costs of voting. These factors lead John Aldrich (1980) to argue "that we should *expect* turnout to be lower . . . for primaries than general elections" (p. 81).

Rather than comparing turnout in primaries to rates of participation in other types of elections, perhaps it would pay to seek an explanation for the variation in turnout across the many presidential primaries. As Figure 3.1 demonstrates, the amount of participation fluctuates widely. For instance, the rate of turnout has ranged from 47.3 percent of eligible voters in Wisconsin (1972) to 4.6 percent in South Dakota (1980).[2] What accounts for these fluctuations? The differing characteristics of the states, such as the level of education of their citizens, may explain them in part. But these variations may also reflect the fact that while some primaries are crucial in choosing a nominee, others are essentially meaningless. The news media and candidates pay more attention to contests that are seen as critical to the selection process, which may increase citizens' interest in them and perhaps raise their chances of participating.[3]

If the variation reflects, in part, the importance of the contest, such a finding would show that the low average turnout in primaries need not reflect badly on voters since many of the contests have little influence in the selection of candidates. A better indicator of participation may then be to calculate turnout in primaries that matter. Perhaps under this new conception turnout will not be viewed as "disappointingly low."

THE VARYING CONDITIONS IN PRESIDENTIAL PRIMARIES

It is very clear that some primaries are more important than others in the selection of candidates. One need only consider the amount of time, energy, and money spent in the New Hampshire primary to realize that not all primaries are equal. But New Hampshire's position as the first primary is not the only source of inequality. Primaries held after a nomination is "sewed up" have little importance to the selection process. For example, once George Bush swept 16 of the 17 contests on Super Tuesday, he was virtually assured of the nomination, making all subsequent primaries of little consequence. Some primaries even in the midst of a competitive struggle for the nomination may be seen as unimportant. In the 1980 Democratic race, for instance, "the presidential candidates [gave] only slight attention to the four May 27th primaries as they [prepared] for the grand finale of the primary season a week later."[4]

Determining which primaries are "important" in the selection of a nominee, then, may help explain the variation in turnout, because voters may be more likely to be interested in a decisive primary. When voters' interest in a primary increases, so do their chances of voting. In the 1980 NES Panel Study, for instance, only 20 percent of those respondents who did not express much interest in the campaign voted, while 55 percent of those who were "very interested" participated in a primary. The same pattern held for the NES's 1988 Super Tuesday study. Therefore, determining which factors influence the "importance" of a primary may help account for the variation in turnout in presidential primaries.

One possible factor that may influence the decisiveness of a primary is the competitiveness of the race. Primaries often are not competitive. Limited resources or dim prospects may lead candidates to ignore a given primary, making it noncompetitive and lowering its interest to voters. On the other hand, a primary may become very competitive if candidates view it as an opportunity to clinch the nomination or to establish themselves as serious contenders for the nomination. A competitive primary generally holds more interest for the electorate, and citizens have a greater incentive to vote in such a contest because they see their votes as playing a greater role in the selection of a nominee. Competitiveness, however, is not just a function of that particular primary but also of the nomination contest as a whole. If an individual primary is competitive but the nomination contest is not, then it is unlikely that that primary will be seen as important. Thus one should examine the competitiveness both of the individual primary and of the nomination in general to provide an accurate indication of competitiveness.[5]

Coverage by the news media and campaign spending by the candidates should also indicate the importance of a primary. Campaign spending by candidates in a state often reflects the significance they attach to a given primary.[6] If candidates view a particular contest as important to their chances, the electorate is likely to also view this contest as more interesting, increasing their likelihood of voting. The news media responding, in part, to the actions of candidates and also their own assessments of the situation, cover more heavily those primaries that are viewed by themselves and candidates as important. With additional media coverage, citizens are likely to be more aware of the contest and its importance.[7]

The number of candidates may also affect the rate of turnout. As the number of candidates increases, the likelihood of a citizen finding one candidate attractive rises. If an individual finds one particular candidate attractive, he or she is more likely to vote (Moran and Fenster 1982; Norrander and Smith 1985). A large field of candidates could, however, confuse partisans, lowering turnout. While that alternative hypothesis may be accurate, voters may respond to large numbers of candidates by focusing on only a few of them and thus, in effect, ignoring the rest of them. The low name-recognition of many of the declared candidates is consistent with the idea that voters do not bother to become familiar with all the contenders.

The interest the electorate might show in a presidential race, however, is not the only thing in a primary that is subject to variation. For instance, the level of education of the electorate varies between primaries since the states differ in the proportion of high school and college graduates. The amount of education citizens possess has been shown to be a powerful predictor of whether they vote in general elections (Wolfinger and Rosenstone 1980). A well-documented fact about turnout in general elections is that "citizens of higher social and economic status participate more in politics. This generalization . . . holds true whether one uses level of education, income, or occupation as the measure of social status" (Verba and Nie 1972, p. 125). Thus, any accurate account of these variations in turnout needs to consider such explanations for voting.

Since 1968 many states have changed from a caucus or a state convention to a direct primary to select delegates. These changes may also help explain these variations in rates of participation. The cost of voting is higher when a state first conducts a primary because there are new rules and regulations with which the voter must become familiar.[8] Such things as having to learn when and where to vote may raise the costs of voting. Moreover, in states that have "established" primaries, many citizens may be in the habit of voting. Whereas, in new primaries voters lack prior experience that may help serve as a reminder to go to the polls.

In short, during the course of the campaign, primaries vary in their importance to the struggle and in their costs of voting for the electorate. With 30 or so primaries in a single campaign, the factors influencing turnout are bound to fluctuate. These changes will not only occur within an election year but also between election years. Each nomination contest will be different, for instance, because in one year a clear front-runner may emerge, while in another year no front-runner may appear. In 1984 the Democratic nomination was competitive, which appeared to stimulate turnout.[9] In contrast, the 1984 Republican primaries had a much lower rate of turnout than the Democratic contests, reflecting the inevitable Reagan renomination. I shall therefore consider variations in turnout that might occur within an election year as well as between election years.

The hypotheses posited above suggest that a model of turnout for presidential primaries should include the following variables: campaign spending, whether the primary is new or not, competitiveness, media attention, the number of candidates in a primary, and level of education in the state.[10] I have therefore constructed the following equation:[11]

Percentage of Turnout = a + b1 (education) + b2 (media attention) + b3 (competitiveness of primary) + b4 (competitiveness of nomination) + b5 (campaign spending) + b6 (new primary) + b7 (number of candidates) + b8 (year) + b9 (party) + E

DATA

Before I can test this model I must decide how to measure turnout in primaries. Previous scholars have relied on at least four different ways to estimate turnout (see Norrander 1986a). For this chapter I shall use data on party registration by state that are available for the 1976 and 1980 presidential primaries.[12] Such data are much more useful than figures on voting-age population (VAP) or registered voters (RV) in the state, which are often the data used in studying turnout. Since primaries are intraparty struggles it is better to use the respective party electorates as the denominator in calculations of turnout.[13] In any given state the electorate includes Democrats, Republicans, and independents. Republicans and independents, for example, may have little interest in voting in a Democratic primary.[14] Being able to define accurately the eligible electorate provides a much better gauge of actual rates of participation because including uninterested (and often ineligible) citizens in the party electorate inflates its size. With this larger eligible electorate the rate of participation declines, further adding to the perception of low turnout in primaries. In addition, these data allow each party's primary to be treated as a separate contest. When using VAP or RV as the denominator, the data are broken down by state, not by each party's contest within the state.[15] Thus by using the denominator I propose, one can examine the different rates of turnout for the two major parties (Ranney 1977, p. 23).[16]

The data concerning party registration, however, have two disadvantages. First, "open" primaries must be excluded from my analysis. In an open primary any registered voter, regardless of party, can participate. I do, however, include primaries that permit independents to vote. In these cases independents are divided equally and added to the number of registered Democratic and Republican voters. By making this adjustment I increase the sample size and include important states such as New Hampshire and Massachusetts. The second drawback is that data on registered party voters do not allow one to consider the effects of registration laws on turnout. Registration laws have been shown to be an important impediment to voting in general elections (Kelley et al. 1967; Wolfinger and Rosenstone 1980). There is, however, some evidence that registration laws play less of a role in primary elections (Jewell 1977).

THE RESULTS

As Table 3.1 shows, attention by the news media and the level of education in the state have a consistent and statistically significant effect on turnout.[17] An increase of 1 percentage point in a state's proportion of high school graduates increases turnout by 1.2 percent. Media attention also appears to have an important effect. If a primary rises from the fourth to the third most covered, turnout increases by over 1 percent. Overall, if a state leaps from the least covered to the most covered, turnout should increase by about 18 percent—a sizable jump. Competitiveness, on the other hand, has a weak effect on the vote. The coefficients are small and vary in direction for both the closeness of the particular contest and the closeness in the number of delegates. Campaign spending has a statistically significant effect only in Democratic primaries and in the 1980 primaries.[18] The number of candidates and whether a primary is new or not do not have statistically significant coefficients, though at times they appear to be substantively important. For example,

Table 3.1
Exploring the Causes of Turnout in Presidential Primaries, 1976—1980

Variable	All Cases	1980 only	1976 only	Reps only	Dems only
	Estimate	Estimate	Estimate	Estimate	Estimate
Intercept	-.42#	-.49#	-.46	-.443	-.568$
	(-3.00)	(-3.29)	(-1.58)	(-1.94)	(-2.52)
Education	.012#	.012#	.013#	.013#	.013#
	(7.06)	(6.27)	(4.18)	(4.81)	(5.41)
Media Attention	.013#	.015#	.017$	.011	.016#
	(3.86)	(4.20)	(2.43)	(1.74)	(3.84)
Competitive Primary	*-.001	.001	*-.001	.001	-.001
	(-.03)	(1.40)	(-.17)	(.59)	(-.80)
Competitive Nomination	*-.001	.001	*-.001	-.001	*.001
	(-.21)	(.85)	(-.11)	(-.50)	(.29)
Campaign Spending@	-.013	-.033#	.023	.010	-.033$
	(-1.11)	(-2.94)	(.83)	(.35)	(2.27)
Number of Candidates	.017	-.021	-.010	-.009	.020
	(1.25)	(-.89)	(-.36)	(-.20)	(1.24)
New Primary	-.003	-.032	.070	-.023	-.001
	(-.10)	(-1.09)	(.93)	(-.40)	(-.02)
Year	-.09#	--	--	-.074	-.122#
	(-3.63)			(-1.04)	(-3.21)
Party	-.04#	-.132#	.006	--	--
	(-1.53)	(-3.31)	(.10)		
	R-Sq=.72	R-Sq=.80	R-Sq=.69	R-Sq=.71	R-Sq=.82
	n=59	n=33	n=26	n=29	n=30

#significant at 99%
$significant at 95%

All estimates are from Ordinary Least Squares regression.
Definitions of these variables are in Appendix 1.

@This variable is the log of spending/voter
*Coefficients are smaller than .001
Figures in Parentheses are T-tests.

Source: Compiled by author.

when using all cases, an additional candidate raises the turnout by almost 2 percent.

The party variable suggests a possible difference in turnout between Democratic and Republican primaries. While the coefficient is not statistically significant at the .05 level, Democratic primaries appear to have 4 percentage points lower turnout than Republicans. In 1976 there was little difference between the parties. When looking at the 1980 primaries only, however, there is a significant difference between the Democrats and the Republicans. GOP primaries had 13 percentage points higher turnout. This latter finding should not be surprising since one might expect higher turnout in Republican primaries. Supporters of the Republican party tend to be better educated than their Democratic counterparts. Republican candidates also spend more per voter than Democratic candidates: each Republican candidate spent $0.21 per party voter, while each Democratic candidate spent $0.13 per party voter.

There is also a significant difference between turnout in the 1976 and 1980 primaries. Turnout was 9 percent lower in 1980 than in 1976. What accounts for such a drop in participation? The news media generally focus on the early primaries and the big industrial states (Robinson and Sheehan 1983). And since these contests are generally the same ones every four years, it is unlikely that changes in the media's coverage could account for such a decrease. The level of education in a state is also unlikely to vary much in a four-year period. Besides, the amount of education among the entire population is going up, not down. Competitiveness, however, can vary. The 1976 primaries were more competitive than the 1980 primaries. In 1976, on average, 20 percent of the vote separated the top two candidates, while in 1980 the difference was over 30 percent. Campaign spending was also lower in 1980. The median spending level was $0.61 per voter for 1976 and only $0.26 per voter for 1980, and these figures do not even reflect inflation. In addition, there were five more new primaries in 1980 than in 1976. In sum, the differences between the level of turnout in 1980 and 1976 may reflect, at least in part, the different campaigns, not that primaries are suffering declining rates of turnout because of a declining interest on the part of the electorate.

Though my model accounts for much of the variation in turnout (R-squared = .72), there is a potential problem when estimating it: many of the independent variables are correlated with each other, resulting in multicollinearity and depressed t-scores. Consequently there may be a significant effect, but multicollinearity prevents the variable from appearing statistically significant. This tangle of effects is especially true for those variables assessing the "importance" of a contest.[19] While attention by the news media has the strongest effect, the strength of its effect is related to the other variables that measure importance. When the news media decide which contests to cover, they consider the importance of the contest to the selection process. As Weaver et al. (1981) observe, "three criteria come to mind that might pre-dispose a news organization to give coverage to a series of delegate selecting events: the number of delegates at stake, the competitiveness of the race, and uncertainty about the outcome" (p. 69). Thus, the strong effect of media attention may reflect indirectly the influence of these other variables. To demonstrate this relationship I estimated the following model:

Media Attention = a + b1 (competitiveness of the primary) + b2 (competitiveness of the nomination) + b3 (campaign spending) + b4 (number of delegates at stake) + b5 (date of the contest) + E

Campaign spending provides an indication of how important the candidates think the race is. The news media, when deciding how to cover each primary, estimate how important the candidates consider these contests to be to their own chances (Arterton 1984). The date of the contest was included since many commentators argue that the news media focus a great deal of attention on the earlier contests, especially New Hampshire's.

Table 3.2 reports the results of this regression. All but one of these variables help account for the news media's coverage of a primary. For example, about 33 additional delegates would move a state from the fourth most covered to the third most covered contest. More campaign spending also brings more coverage by the news media. The competitiveness of the specific race, however, appears to have little effect on media attention, though as the competitiveness of the overall contest for the nomination increases, the news media's coverage of that primary also increases.

Given the results in Tables 3.1 and 3.2, a simpler model of turnout seems appropriate. Since some of the variables posited at the outset seem to have little explanatory value and since media attention appears to be a good surrogate for the "importance" of a primary, I estimated the following model:

Percentage of registered party members voting = a + b1 (education) + b2 (media attention) + b3 (year) + b4 (party) + E

The results of this regression are reported in Table 3.3. As one can see, the percentage of variance explained, .70, remains high. The coefficients indicate that in states with a well-educated electorate and a heavily covered primary, turnout should be about 69 percent.[20] On the other hand, turnout in an unimportant primary in a state with a relatively poorly educated citizenry falls to 30 percent.[21] This 39 percentage point gap is consistent with the large variation in turnout we witnessed in Figure 3.1.

Table 3.2
**Explaining the News Media's Attention in Presidential Primaries,
1976–1980**

Variable$	Coefficient	T-Score
Intercept	4.73#	2.42
Competitiveness of Primary	-.01	-.52
Competitiveness of Nomination	.04##	2.19
Campaign Spending@	.75#	2.88
Number of Delegates at Stake	.03#	6.61
Order of the Primary	-.31#	3.96

R-squared=.66
n=59

#Significant at 99%
##Significant at 95%

The dependent variable ranges from 1 to 15, with 15 signifying
the most-covered contest and 1 the least-covered contest. Thus,
a positive slope for a variable indicates that an increase of one
unit in the independent variable increases the amount of media
coverage.

@Campaign spending is the log of (total spent per number of
registered partisans).
$See Appendix I for description of variables.

CONCLUDING OBSERVATIONS

What do these results suggest about participation in presidential primaries? First, the fluctuations in turnout in the state primaries reflect, in
large part, the importance of the contest. As a primary becomes more
decisive, turnout increases. These findings suggest that the variation in
turnout in presidential primaries reflects an electorate that, in part, responds to the importance of each contest. In the 1976 Florida Republican primary, for example, 61 percent of the registered party electorate
voted. This figure stands in contrast to the 1980 Kentucky Democratic
contest where about 18 percent of eligible party voters participated. While
one cannot argue that this 43 percentage point gap solely reflects the

Table 3.3
Explaining the Proportion of Turnout in Presidential Primaries,
1976-1980

Variable$	Coefficient	T-Score
Intercept	-.347#	-3.38
Education	.012#	7.63
Media Attention	.012#	4.62
Year of Primary	-.090#	-4.34
Party	-.022	-1.13
	R-squared = .70	
	n=59	

#Significant at 99%

$See Appendix I for description of variables.
Coefficients are rounded off to the third decimal place.

fact that the Florida race was seen as more important to the prospects of the candidates than Kentucky's contest, a sizable part of it can be nonetheless explained by such forces. In fact, given the regression estimates in Table 3.3, turnout should typically be over 60 percent in those states with the greatest amount of news media coverage, while for states with little media attention, turnout will fall to 46 percent.[22] As hypothesized at the outset, "significant" primaries generate higher rates of turnout than "nonsignificant" primaries, indicating that the average rate of participation is deceiving. Therefore, turnout in primaries may not be "disappointingly low" as scholars often contend, providing that politicians and journalists focus attention on the contest.

The fact that some participants appear to respond to the conditions present in that primary suggests they may be more aware of the campaign for the presidential nomination of their party than many critics believe. If so, electorates in primaries may be more informed than these critics contend. Of course, the data presented here can only hint at such a conclusion. Consequently, we now turn to the question of whether voters in primaries are informed.

NOTES

1. The amount of information, however, increases as the nomination process unfolds, which could lower the cost in later primaries. Patterson (1980), Brady and Johnston (1987), and Bartels (1988) show that the public's awareness of candidates increases as the campaign proceeds.

2. Turnout varies much more in primaries than in general elections. The standard deviation of the VAP turnout in primaries from 1972 to 1988 was 9. In contrast, the VAP turnout by state in the 1984 presidential election had a standard deviation of 6.5.

3. Jack Moran and Mark Fenster (1982) and Barbara Norrander and Gregg Smith (1985) make similar points, arguing that the "primary environment" has an important effect on turnout.

4. The passage cited is from *Congressional Quarterly Weekly Report*, May 17th, 1980, p. 7. The four primaries were held in Arkansas, Idaho, Kentucky, and Nevada.

5. Lawrence Rothenberg and Richard Brody (1988) come to a similar conclusion, arguing that the "electoral stakes" in a primary affect turnout. "Electoral stakes" can be either the closeness of the particular primary or the overall contest for the nomination.

6. Campaign spending may also lessen information costs for the voter. With additional campaign funds the electorate should be more familiar with the candidates since, presumably, part of this money will buy more advertisements. Visits may also lessen costs because the electorate will see more of the candidate, whether in person or through the news media's coverage of the visit.

7. Patterson (1980) offers support for this contention by showing that additional coverage by the news media increases the electorate's interest in the campaign.

8. Richard Rubin (1980) develops the idea that turnout "must be adjusted for 'new' and 'old' primary states" (p. 134). However, he limits the discussion to differences between turnout in general and primary elections. Patrick Kenney and Tom Rice (1985) also include a variable that tests for differences in turnout among "traditional" primaries.

9. The share of voters increased by 18.8 percent in 1984 over 1980 for the early primaries, according to *The Congressional Quarterly Weekly Report*, April 7th, 1984, p. 772.

10. One might argue that the date of the primary is an important variable since the earlier contests are likely to be of more interest. The problem, however, is that the date of the primary is not a separate independent variable but instead another way to look at competitiveness, campaign spending, and media attention. In addition, the actual effect of this variable may vary between nomination contests. If a front-runner emerges from the pack at the outset of the campaign, later primaries may be seen as unimportant. On the other hand, if no front-runner emerges, the latter contests become more important. Thus even if there is an independent effect, it is likely to depend directly on the particular circumstances of that contest.

11. See Appendix I for definitions of the variables in the equation.

12. Data on party registration are not available for 1984. While they are available for 1988, the measures of some of the relevant independent variables are not. So I must focus on the primaries in 1976 and 1980.

13. Rothenberg and Brody (1988) use "a moving average of the partisan division of the vote in the previous three congressional elections" (pp. 257–58). This measure provides a better base line than RV or VAP, but it is still not as good as registered party voters, as Rothenberg and Brody suggest.

14. Patterson (1980) supports the idea that partisans are more interested in their party's nomination contest than in the other intraparty struggle.

15. See Ranney (1977) or Mark Wattier (1983c) for examples of a state-by-state breakdown of turnout in primaries.

16. Norrander (1986a) advocates the use of the normal vote as the denominator. While this measure has advantages, it does not precisely estimate how many citizens are in fact eligible to participate in a primary.

17. These data only refer to 1976 and 1980. Some supporting evidence can be found in 1988, however. "Media attention" is also correlated with turnout of registered party voters in 1988 (r = .32). In this case, attention by the news media was measured by counting the number of stories about a state's primary in the *Christian Science Monitor* and the *New York Times* Index. This is a rough indicator, but it lends further support to the notion that as the news media's coverage grows, so does the rate of turnout.

18. Another variable that could also measure how important candidates view a primary is the number of visits they make to that state. Such data, however, are available only for 1976 (see Aldrich 1980). When holding other variables, such as education, constant, it appears that for every ten additional visits by candidates, turnout increases by about 8 percent—a quite significant effect.

19. One way to minimize the problem of multicollinearity is to test for the aggregate effect of these variables on turnout. An F-test can determine if competitiveness, campaign spending, and media attention together have a statistically significant effect on turnout. The F-test score for these variables is 7.27, which is significant at the .01 level. Thus, the aggregate effect of the "importance" variables is statistically significant. This test, however, tells us that there is an effect, but how much of an effect remains unclear.

20. This figure assumes the percentage of citizens who have a high school education to be 75. For instance, around 75 percent of the citizens of California and Oregon had a high school education. The amount of media attention is 15—the highest rating in my scale.

21. The result assumes that 55 percent of a state's citizens have a high school education. About 55 percent of the citizens of Kentucky and North Carolina had completed 12 years of school. The amount of media attention is 1—the lowest on my scale.

22. To estimate these proportions I used the average education level for the states studied. Of course, a state with a higher-than-average level of education would have even greater participation, while the reverse is also true.

===4===

Information and Voters in Presidential Primaries

Over two hundred years ago the Founding Fathers doubted the ability of the electorate to select good presidents. A major fear was that people would not be well enough informed to choose candidates wisely.[1] In a slightly different form, that concern still exists. A number of scholars question whether voters in primaries possess sufficient information to nominate good candidates (see, for instance, Marshall 1981; Weaver et al. 1981). Marshall (1983), for example, contends that presidential primaries take place in a "climate of . . . poorly informed public opinion" (p. 60). Keeter and Zukin (1983) go so far as to title their book about the current nominating system *Uninformed Choice*.

Such assessments, however, often do not consider carefully enough the standards by which we should judge the information possessed by voters in primaries. That is, how do we know when voters are "informed"? Certainly if voters knew all the views and qualifications of the candidates running in a primary, we could confidently claim that voters are "informed." But all voters, and not just those who participate in primaries, fail to meet that standard. By using this tough standard to decide whether voters are informed or not, one could easily conclude that the electorate should neither nominate nor elect public officials. Therefore, unless we want to question the entire election process, we should not expect voters in primaries to be completely informed about the candidates. The question becomes, then, what alternative criteria to use when making this difficult judgment. If voters, for instance, know three out of the six contenders for the nomination, does that mean they are informed or uninformed? What if they know all three of the "serious" candidates, but none of the three "dark horses." Does that make

them more informed? If voters only learn about candidates with ideological leanings similar to their own, does that suggest they are informed?
These kinds of questions point to the problem of deciding whether voters in primaries are ''informed'' or ''uninformed.''

This chapter seeks to establish a set of standards to assess the information voters in primaries possess. Having done so, I shall then present
some data about the information voters possess concerning candidates
who compete in presidential primaries. But first I shall raise a problem
with much of the previous research on this matter.

A PROBLEM FACING THE PREVIOUS RESEARCH

One of the major problems in examining the information voters in primaries possess concerns the lack of good data. Bartels (1988) and Brady
and Johnston (1987), for instance, make use of the NES's continuous
monitoring survey in 1984. Keeter and Zukin (1983) rely on the NES's
surveys in 1980 and polls for the Eagleton Institute in New Jersey. Marshall (1981) examines results from the Gallup Polls of the national electorate. While each of these sources sheds light on what the public knows
about candidates for nomination, none of them provides direct insights
about how well informed the actual *voters* in primaries are. It is the
latter group we are concerned about.

Any conclusions from surveys of the national electorate may be problematic because these respondents may possess vastly different amounts
of information than a sample of actual voters in a primary. Polls of the
national electorate contain only a handful of people who are about to
vote in a presidential primary. Most respondents, therefore, will not have
had the benefit of a campaign. During a campaign potential voters in
primaries will come across not only the political advertising of the candidates but also a good deal of coverage of the candidates by *local* television, radio, and newspapers. These sources of information may help
voters learn about the candidates and what they stand for. This information should be especially critical for candidates who are not well known
to the public. In addition, potential voters in a state with an upcoming
primary may be more interested in the candidates, knowing they have
an opportunity to vote in the near future. Citizens in other states may
lack this interest, further widening the gap between voters in primaries
and those in the national electorate. Consequently, findings about what
the national electorate knows about the candidates may greatly underestimate what voters in particular primaries know about the contenders.

Data from the NES's Super Tuesday study clearly support this hypothesis. Among Democratic identifiers in the Super Tuesday states, 9.2
percent claimed to know a ''fair amount'' or ''quite a lot'' about Gore,
Dukakis, Gephardt, and Jackson, the four major contenders for the nom-

ination. When examining just voters, more than *twice* that proportion said they knew a "fair amount" or "quite a lot" about these four contenders. The same pattern holds for the Republicans. About 13 percent of Republican identifiers did not know much about *any* of the four major contenders (Bush, Dole, Kemp, and Robertson). Among voters, however, the proportion declines to 7 percent. If one looks at other kinds of information, like the respondents' knowledge of the contenders' chances and ideological positions, the same pattern holds. In short, as expected, voters in primaries are quite a bit more informed than party identifiers.

The differences cited above actually *understate* the gap between the information of voters in primaries and party identifiers. First, the partisans surveyed in 1988 lived in states with primaries, making it a regional sample. With a national survey of partisans, the differences may have been even greater since respondents in states with primaries are more likely to come across information about candidates than respondents in states without these intraparty struggles. Second, the preelection wave of the Super Tuesday study was conducted between January 17th and March 8th. Many of the interviews, therefore, were conducted before the New Hampshire primary. Those pre–New Hampshire respondents may not have been paying much attention to the campaign because the candidates' attention had been focused on Iowa and New Hampshire. Thus at the time of the interview, voters may have had less information than when they actually entered the polling booth on March 8th. Results from the Super Tuesday study confirm this latter argument. Among all Democratic voters, 28 percent could estimate Gore's, Dukakis's, Gephardt's, and Jackson's ideological positions. For those voters interviewed after the New Hampshire primary, the proportion swells to about 37 percent. A similar pattern exists for Republicans. The results also hold for other matters like voters' awareness of the candidates and their chances of winning.[2]

In an attempt to overcome this problem facing previous research, I will rely only on data about voters in primaries. My data, however, are not without fault. Some of the surveys I use were not conducted right before an actual primary. This problem is especially true for the NES data from 1980, which took interviews in January and June. In January, voters have had little opportunity to learn about all the contenders. By June, voters have had great opportunity to become acquainted with the candidates, but the actual primaries have long since passed. Consequently, without the heat of a campaign the June survey may also skew the information of voters. Fortunately, the NES 1988 Super Tuesday study and Patterson's 1976 study interviewed respondents around the time of a presidential primary, so most of the data should be quite reliable.[3]

ESTABLISHING BENCHMARKS

Answering the question of whether voters in primaries are informed depends heavily on the definition of "informed." Some scholars, for instance, may think that voters should be acquainted with all the contenders for the nomination. Others may prefer a less stringent standard. So, for instance, if voters know four of five candidates or four of six contenders, does that make them "informed"? Choosing between these kinds of standards borders on being arbitrary because it is not clear at what point voters become "informed." Rather than setting up an absolute standard for determining how well informed voters in primaries are, perhaps they should be judged on a relative basis. That is, we might compare the information of voters in primaries to that of voters in other elections. Specifically, citizens who participate in presidential elections might serve as a useful benchmark.[4] While there may be complaints that voters in these elections are not as well informed as would be desired, rarely do critics argue that they should be prevented from participating because of a lack of information.

One may argue, however, that the choice facing voters in primaries is more difficult than that in general elections. As Keeter and Zukin (1983) observe, "there are more candidates for the voter to become familiar with and party labels are unable to provide informational cues or serve as a screening mechanism" (p. 60). In addition, voters in general elections have had the benefit of at least five months of extra campaigning. Consequently, using general elections as a base of comparison may be an unfair standard for assessing the information of voters in primaries. But if voters in primaries are as well informed as participants in the presidential contest, such a finding would suggest that they have overcome these potential obstacles. It should be reasonable, therefore, to conclude that they are "informed."

There are, however, other problems that face using voters in presidential elections as the benchmark. First, in many primaries large numbers of candidates compete. Yet in the November election, there are usually only two major contenders. Occasionally, a serious third-party candidate will run, like John Anderson or George Wallace. But when more than three candidates compete in a primary, the general election loses its value as a benchmark. A second problem is that while knowing the candidates' chances for success is important in contests for the nomination, such information has little relevance in the general election. This latter problem further undercuts the value of using the general election as a benchmark. The problems become, first, how to assess the information of voters in primaries when four or more candidates compete, and second, how to judge whether voters know the candidates' chances for the nomination. These questions have no straightforward answers, given my contention that some reasonable standard should be used to judge voters' information. I shall, nonetheless, present evidence about these cases, trying to be cautious in reaching any overall conclusion.

When deciding whether voters in primaries are "informed," we also need to consider what information they should possess. Such things as assessments of the candidates themselves and knowledge of the candidates' views on issues and their ideological affiliations would all seem to be necessary for voters to make good choices. Without such information voters would be more likely to choose candidates who espouse different views from themselves or to choose candidates who might prove to be weak leaders. In addition, the decision-makers should be aware of the candidates' chances for winning the nomination and general election, since electability is an important concern when deciding on who to support for the nomination.

One final problem when assessing the information of voters concerns some estimate of the quality of information, not just the quantity. This latter judgment is fraught with danger, because deciding what constitutes good information is extremely difficult. Someone might, for instance, reasonably rate Dukakis as a conservative. At first this judgment appears flawed, but if that individual is extremely left-wing, Dukakis could well appear to be conservative. There is, however, a safer way to assess the quality of information. Voters in primaries, for instance, should in the aggregate rate Gore as more conservative than Jackson. Or voters should assess Mondale's prospects in 1984 as better than Cranston's. These kinds of comparisons may shed some light on whether these participants are making reasonable judgments about the candidates.

INFORMATION ABOUT CANDIDATES

The results in Table 4.1 indicate that in contests with just two competitors, voters in primaries appear as likely to have said that they "know something" about the candidates as voters in presidential elections. For instance, in Erie, Pennsylvania, about 90 percent of voters in *both* the primary and general election said they knew something about the two contenders. The same pattern is true for the other two cases. In fact, more voters in Los Angeles knew Reagan and Ford than Carter and Ford, probably reflecting Reagan's status as the former governor of California.

While the above evidence bodes well for voters in primaries, problems begin to surface once the field of candidates increases. Since the November contest is rarely contested by more than two serious contenders, using general-election voters as a base of comparison is problematic, as noted above. We can, nevertheless, examine three-candidate races, comparing the 1980 general election to the battle among Anderson, Bush,

Table 4.1
The Number of Contenders Known by Voters in Presidential Primaries

Two-Candidate Races:

	Democratic Primaries January '80	General Election '80
Number of Candidates		
Zero	0%	.3%
One	1.9%	.8%
Two	98.1%	98.9%
N	159	996

	Republican Primary Erie, Pa. '76	General Election Erie, Pa. '76
Number of Candidates		
Zero	2.7%	5.5%
One	5.5%	4.7%
Two	91.8%	89.8%
N	73	384

	Republican Primary L.A., Ca. '76	General Election L.A., Ca. '76
Number of Candidates		
Zero	0%	2.0%
One	0%	1.2%
Two	100%	96.8%
N	82	251

Three-Candidate Races:

	Republican Primaries June '80	General Election '80
Number of Candidates		
Zero	1.1%	.2%
One	14.0%	.6%
Two	23.7%	6.3%
Three	61.3%	92.9%
N	93	996

Source: Patterson's 1976 panel study and NES 1980 panel and general election studies.

and Reagan. While at the outset there were more than three contenders in that GOP struggle, the winnowing process cut short the candidacies of people like Dole and Baker. As shown in Table 4.1, the comparison of these contests demonstrates that voters in general elections are more likely to know all three contenders than are voters in primaries. Still, however, 85 percent of voters in Republican primaries knew at least two of the three contenders. But since these voters were interviewed in June, these proportions may be in error. Anderson and Bush had both faded from the contest for the nomination by May. With a more competitive contest, it is possible that these proportions might have been higher. But in any case it probably would not have been as high as in the general election.

Of course, many primaries have more than three candidates competing, especially at the outset of the campaign. While using general-election voters as a base of comparison is of little value in this case, I shall present evidence only about voters in primaries when a large number of candidates competes. As one might expect, many voters were not aware of all the candidates in a large field. For instance, only 41 percent of voters in Los Angeles said they knew something about the four major contenders in that Democratic primary, though 80 percent knew at least something about two of the contenders. In 1988 on the Republican side, about two-thirds of voters knew all four contenders. Among Democratic voters that year, about 47 percent claimed to know at least "a little" about Gore, Jackson, Gephardt, and Dukakis. Less than 4 percent of Democratic voters knew nothing about any of the four contenders. Keep in mind that these percentages may underestimate the actual information of voters, since nearly all the interviews took place before the day of the primary. For instance, about 87 percent of Democratic voters who knew two or fewer candidates were interviewed prior to the last weekend before Super Tuesday. The proportion is about the same for voters in the GOP's primaries. It is possible that these voters may have picked up additional information in the waning days of the campaign. This is obviously an optimistic interpretation of the data, but it is at least possible.

In general, the findings in Tables 4.1 and 4.2 present a mixed picture. In two-candidate races, voters in primaries seem well acquainted with the candidates, assuming one accepts my comparison of voters in primaries to voters in general elections. This tendency, however, appears to be less true as the number of contestants grows. Of course, these data only speak to whether voters said they "knew something" about the candidates—a weak test of voters' information. In the next section I shall examine whether voters in primaries are aware of the positions candidates take on issues.

Table 4.2
The Number of Contenders Known by Voters in Presidential
Primaries in Large-Candidate Fields

Democratic Primaries, 1976

Number of Candidates	Erie, Pa.#	Los Angeles, Ca.#
Zero	8.7%	1.4%
One	10.7%	4.3%
Two	22.8%	30.5%
Three	25.5%	22.7%
Four	32.2%	41.1%
N	149	141

Republican Primaries, 1980*

Number of Candidates	January
Zero	0
One	10.8%
Two	16.1%
Three	14.0%
Four	22.6%
Five	25.8%
Six	10.8%
N	93

Super Tuesday, 1988

Number of Candidates	Republicans	Democrats
Zero	1.0%	3.8%
One	3.8%	13.7%
Two	6.7%	15.1%
Three	22.1%	20.3%
Four	66.3%	47.2%
N	104	212

*The six candidates were Reagan, Connally, Bush, Dole, Crane and Baker.
#In Erie, the four candidates were Henry Jackson, Wallace, Carter and Udall. In Los Angeles, Frank Church and Jerry Brown replaced Jackson and Wallace. These sets of candidates were used in all the following analyses.

Source: Patterson's 1976 panel study, NES 1980 and 1988 panel and general election studies.

INFORMATION ABOUT ISSUES

In two-candidate races, voters in general elections were more aware of the candidates' views on issues than were voters in primaries (see Table 4.3). For instance, about 61 percent of primary voters in Erie said they knew both candidates' views on the five issues examined. In the

Table 4.3
The Information Voters in Presidential Primaries Possess About Contenders' Views on Issues in Two-Candidate Contests[$]

Number of Issues	Democratic Voters in Primaries, January '80		General Election '80	
	Libcon	Others#	Libcon	Others
Zero	24.5%	11.2%	31.9%	26.1%
One	1.9%	13.4%	4.6%	11.7%
Two	73.6%	74.4%	63.5%	62.2%
	N = 159		N = 996	

Republican Voters in Primaries:
Erie, Pa. (1976)

Number of Issues	Tax	Def-Sp.	Jobs	Busing	Welfare	Libcon
Zero	28.8%	16.4%	27.4%	27.4%	26.0%	13.7%
One	12.3%	12.3%	12.3%	19.2%	12.3%	9.6%
Two	58.9%	71.2%	60.3%	53.4%	61.6%	76.9%
	N = 73					

Voters in General Election:
Erie, Pa. (1976)

Number of Issues	Tax	Def-Sp.	Jobs	Busing	Welfare	Libcon
Zero	14.1%	15.9%	19.3%	21.6%	17.7%	15.9%
One	10.9%	9.6%	10.7%	10.2%	8.3%	5.2%
Two	75.0%	74.5%	70.1%	68.2%	74.0%	78.9%
	N = 384					

Republican Voters in Primaries:
Los Angeles, Ca. (1976)

Number of Issues	Tax	Def-Sp.	Jobs	Busing	Welfare	Libcon
Zero	31.7%	13.4%	30.5%	15.9%	14.6%	8.5%
One	0 %	3.7%	3.7%	6.1%	4.9%	1.2%
Two	68.3%	82.9%	65.9%	78.0%	80.5%	90.2%
	N = 82					

Voters in General Election:
Los Angeles, Ca. (1976)

Number of Issues	Tax	Def-Sp.	Jobs	Busing	Welfare	Libcon
Zero	10.8%	12.0%	11.2%	14.7%	16.8%	7.6%
One	8.4%	3.2%	6.0%	10.4%	6.8%	5.2%
Two	80.9%	84.9%	82.9%	74.9%	82.5%	87.3%
	N = 251					

[$]See Appendix II for actual questions used.
#"Others" is an average of the closed-ended questions about issues in the survey. An average was used because different questions were asked in the various surveys, making direct comparisons difficult.
Source: Patterson's 1976 panel study and NES 1980 panel and general election studies.

general election, the percentage was about 72. In Los Angeles there was less of a difference between voters in primaries and general-election voters, though the latter was still, on average, better informed about the candidates' views on these five issues. But as noted before, this narrower gap is surely due to Reagan's familiarity to voters in California.

Participants in primaries appear about as familiar with candidates' liberal-conservative positions as voters in general elections. In Patterson's study of Erie and Los Angeles, for instance, voters in both elections appear equally likely to know the candidates' liberal-conservative stances. In June 1980, 23.3 percent of voters in Democratic primaries could not place either Carter or Kennedy on the liberal-conservative scale. In the 1980 presidential election, 31.9 percent of voters could not place either Carter or Reagan on that scale. If one views the liberal-conservative spectrum as a rough proxy for views on issues, this evidence bodes well for voters in primaries.

In three-candidate contests, I shall again rely on the 1980 general election for purposes of comparison. The electorate in the 1980 Republican primaries had amounts of information slightly less than those who have voted in presidential elections (see Table 4.4). About 54 percent of voters in the general election said they knew all three candidates' liberal-conservative positions, while about 47 percent of voters in Republican primaries did. A similar difference exists when examining voters' information about the candidates' views on issues. For instance, about 21 percent of voters in primaries knew none of the candidates' views on defense spending. The proportion in the general election is about 15.

In the second part of the table I present data for races where four candidates compete. In general, about 15 to 20 percent of voters in Erie and Los Angeles knew the four candidates' views on issues. The overall trend, which was pointed to in Table 4.2, is that as the number of candidates increases, voters are less likely to be familiar with all the contenders. The same pattern held in 1988, where voters were asked to estimate the contenders' liberal-conservative stances. Among Democratic voters, 35.8 percent were able to place Jackson, Dukakis, Gore, and Gephardt on the traditional seven-point scale. Over a quarter of the voters, however, did not know any of the four contenders' position on the liberal-conservative spectrum. For Republicans the proportion of well-informed voters is quite a bit higher. Nearly 56 percent of voters surveyed after New Hampshire's primary estimated Bush's, Dole's, Kemp's, and Robertson's ideological positions.

Voters in primaries are not as well acquainted with the contenders' ideological leanings as one would prefer, but the perceptions of those voters who could estimate the candidates' positions appear reasonably accurate. In the Democratic camp, Gore was viewed as the most conservative and Jackson as the most liberal. For instance, 46 percent of

Table 4.4

The Information Voters in Presidential Primaries Possess About Contenders' Views on Issues in Multicandidate Contests

Three-Candidate Race:
Republican Primaries, 1980#

Number of Issues	Libcon	Def-Sp.	Gov-Sp.	Infla.
Zero	18.3%	21.5%	25.8%	32.3%
One	12.9%	21.5%	14.0%	17.2%
Two	21.5%	25.8%	22.6%	18.3%
Three	47.3%	31.2%	37.6%	32.3%

N = 92

General Election: 1980$

Number of Issues	Libcon	Def-Sp.	Gov-Sp.	Infla.
Zero	31.8%	14.5%	19.0%	41.8%
One	2.6%	6.7%	8.1%	7.3%
Two	11.9%	30.9%	26.9%	17.8%
Three	53.6%	47.9%	46.0%	33.1%

N = 996

Four-Candidate Race:
Democratic Primary: Erie, Pa. 1976

Number of Issues	Tax	Def-Sp.	Jobs	Busing	Welfare	Libcon
Zero	36.2%	33.6%	38.9%	22.1%	35.6%	21.6%
One	18.1%	13.4%	17.4%	24.2%	16.1%	11.4%
Two	17.4%	20.8%	14.1%	21.5%	16.1%	22.8%
Three	13.4%	14.1%	14.8%	15.4%	14.1%	17.4%
Four	14.8%	18.1%	14.8%	16.8%	18.1%	26.8%

N = 149

Democratic Primary: Los Angeles, Ca. 1976

Number of Issues	Tax	Def-Sp.	Jobs	Busing	Welfare	Libcon
Zero	22.7%	19.9%	17.0%	12.8%	12.1%	5.7%
One	8.5%	7.1%	8.5%	12.1%	12.8%	5.7%
Two	29.1%	28.4%	27.0%	36.2%	31.2%	31.9%
Three	18.4%	17.0%	19.1%	19.1%	19.1%	21.3%
Four	21.3%	27.7%	28.4%	19.9%	24.8%	35.5%

N = 141

Republican Voters in Primaries: January 1980

Number of Issues	Libcon	Def-Sp.	Gov-Sp.	USSR
Zero	31.2%	26.9%	26.9%	26.9%
One	14.0%	9.7%	12.9%	11.8%
Two	15.1%	21.5%	22.6%	19.4%
Three	8.6%	16.1%	12.9%	16.1%
Four	31.2%	25.8%	24.7%	25.8%

N = 92

Table 4.4 Continued

Voters in the Super Tuesday Primaries: 1988		
Number	Republicans	Democrats
Known	Libcon	Libcon
Zero	12.5%	26.4%
One	3.8%	8.5%
Two	9.6%	11.3%
Three	18.3%	17.9%
Four	55.8%	35.8%
N	104	212

#See Appendix II for the actual questions used.

Source: NES 1980 panel and general election studies and 1988
Super Tuesday study and Patterson's 1976 panel study.

voters who estimated Jackson's stance gave him a six or seven on the ideological scale—the two most liberal positions. Among those who placed Gore, only 2.4 percent put him in either of those two categories. Nearly a quarter of those who rated Dukakis placed him in the sixth and seventh slots. Gephardt's proportion was 12.3. Most pundits would concur that Jackson was the most liberal, followed by Dukakis, Gephardt, and Gore. Data from the Republican side tell a similar story. Around 42 percent of voters who claimed to know Bush's ideological stance gave him a one or a two on the scale (the two most conservative positions). Dole was viewed slightly less conservative (about 38 percent). Both Robertson and Kemp were viewed as much more conservative than the two front-runners (about 60 percent). These perceptions are also consistent with the conventional wisdom at the time.

While one can put a positive light on these findings, two conclusions seem quite clear. First, voters in general elections and in primaries have comparable information about the candidates *providing* the number of candidates is small. Second, as the number of candidates grows, the proportion of voters in primaries who know all the candidates' stances on issues dwindles significantly. Whether this decline means that voters are uninformed is less clear, but it is at minimum a cause for concern.

INFORMATION ABOUT THE CHANCES OF CANDIDATES

Being aware of the candidates and their views on the issues is not the only information necessary to make informed political choices. Knowledge of a candidate's prospects for victory at the convention and at the polls in November is important when supporting a candidate for the nomination; voters may otherwise end up "wasting" their votes or choosing candidates unable to compete successfully in November. Table 4.5 presents data concerning the proportion of voters who are aware of the chances of their party's contenders to win both the nomination and general election.

As the table shows, when two candidates compete, voters generally have some idea of the chances of the contenders seeking their party's nomination. In Los Angeles (1976), over 95 percent of Republican identifiers were willing to estimate both Reagan's and Ford's chances for the nomination and general election. In a four-candidate race, over 80 percent of voters in Erie (1976) estimated at least two of the four contenders' chances for the nomination, and 32.2 percent estimated the chances of all four candidates. By the time of the California primary, over 40 percent of voters estimated the chances of all the remaining Democratic contenders. This slight increase is probably due to the additional opportunities voters in California had to learn about the candidates' chances. In 1988, about 65 percent of Republican voters assessed the prospects of the four major contenders for the nomination. Only 2 percent had no guesses on any of the four contenders. In the Democratic camp, 82.2 percent knew two of the four contenders' chances for the nomination.

Interestingly, these estimates of the candidates' chances were reasonably accurate. By the time of the 1976 California primary, the vast majority of voters saw Carter as the likely nominee, with a few respondents holding out hope for Jerry Brown.[5] In 1988, voters saw Bush as the favorite for the nomination with Dole a close second. Robertson was not seen as a likely winner of either the nomination or the general election. While there was more uncertainty on the Democratic side, Dukakis was viewed as the favorite by voters prior to Super Tuesday. Jackson, as one might expect, was viewed as unlikely to win the general election or the nomination. Most pundits held similar views of the 1976 and 1988 contests, suggesting that voters in primaries may be able to estimate with some accuracy the relative chances of the contenders.

CONCLUSION

The evidence presented in this chapter has a number of implications. First, when voters in primaries are faced with a choice between two candidates, they appear as informed as are voters in general elections. While this finding does not necessarily mean that voters in primaries are well enough informed to make good choices, it does suggest that they may be able to do as good a job of selecting a candidate as are voters in general elections. The second and probably more important implication is that as the number of competing candidates increases, the more likely it is that voters will be unfamiliar with all the possible choices facing them. Consequently, in the earlier primaries when there can be a large

Table 4.5

The Information Voters in Presidential Primaries Possess About Contenders' Chances of Winning the Nomination and General Election

---

Voters in Primaries, 1976:

Chances for the Nomination

Number of Candidates	Erie Dem.	Erie Rep.	L.A. Dem.	L.A. Rep.
Zero	8.7%	2.7%	1.4%	1.2%
One	10.7%	6.8%	4.3%	0%
Two	23.5%	90.4%	30.5%	98.8%
Three	24.8%		23.4%	
Four	32.2%		40.4%	
N	149	73	141	82

Chances for the General Election

Number of Candidates	L.A. Dem.	L.A. Rep.
Zero	.7%	0 %
One	.7%	1.2%
Two	98.6%	98.8%
N	141	82

Voters in Primaries, 1988

Chances for the Nomination

Number of Candidates	Democrats	Republicans
Zero	3.8%	1.9%
One	13.7%	3.8%
Two	15.1%	6.7%
Three	20.3%	23.1%
Four	47.2%	64.4%
N	212	104

Chances for the General Election

Number of Candidates	Democrats	Republicans
Zero	4.2%	1.9%
One	13.7%	3.8%
Two	15.6%	6.7%
Three	19.8%	22.1%
Four	46.7%	65.4%
N	212	104

Source: Patterson's 1976 panel study and NES 1988 Super Tuesday study.

field of contenders, voters in primaries seem unlikely to be able to make a decision that considers all active alternatives. Such situations are undesirable since voters may end up overlooking a contender who might have proven to be a good choice.

One could argue that all of this evidence points to the basic conclusion that voters in primaries are not very well informed. While voters may occasionally have amounts of information similar to that of voters in general elections, this finding does not in any way suggest that voters are "informed." Perhaps so. The question, then, becomes whether this finding validates the more general claim of some scholars that voters should be given a reduced role in the nominating process because of their lack of information.

If the objective of a nominating system is to maximize the information of decision-makers, a system that relies on direct primaries to select delegates is inferior to a system that relies on the party leadership to make choices. But, of course, the objective for any nominating system is not simply to have informed decision-makers but rather to choose good candidates consistently. Many scholars believe that having "informed" decision-makers will increase the likelihood that good candidates are chosen. Polsby (1983) makes this point when he contends that "peer review" is important to nominating good candidates because it allows an assessment of "the qualities of candidates for public office according to such dimensions as intelligence, sobriety of judgment, intellectual flexibility, ability to work well with others, willingness to learn from experience, detailed personal knowledge of government, and other personal characteristics which can be best revealed through personal acquaintance" (p. 169).[6] And since voters lack detailed information about the candidates (especially when a large number compete), they are unlikely to choose good candidates on a consistent basis. This reasoning would lead one to advocate reforms that lessen the role of voters in the selection of nominees.

Such a conclusion may, however, be hasty. Party leaders are more informed than voters in primaries, but the former are also more subject to corruption than the latter. If one's objective is to minimize the chance of corruption in a nominating system, then voters in primaries would be preferred over party leaders. And one might argue that with less corruption, the chances of selecting a good candidate increase. Thus the normative criteria one brings to bear in evaluating the system help account for one's assessment of the system. But I think most scholars would agree that the central objective of any nominating system is to select good candidates and that these "sub" goals are simply means to achieve that end. In short, one cannot simply argue that voters in primaries should play less of a role in the selection of nominees because they are not as well informed as party leaders. While such an argument has merit, there are other considerations that determine whether a set of decision-makers can consistently yield good candidates. One consideration is the criteria the decision-makers employ when selecting a candidate—the subject of the next chapter.

NOTES

1. George Mason, for instance, argued at the time of the Constitutional Convention that: "it would be as unnatural to refer the choice of a proper character for Chief Magistrate to the people, as it would, to refer a trial of colours to a blind man. The extent of the country renders it impossible that the people can have requisite capacity to judge of the respective pretensions of the candidates." This passage is taken from Lucius Wilmerding (1958), p. 5.

2. Interestingly, these findings may help explain why the electoral prospects of the contenders appear to be so important to some theories of voting in primaries (see Bartels 1988; Brady and Johnston 1987). A national sample of partisans may be familiar mostly with the chances of the candidates since their information is primarily the "horse race" from the national media. Thus those respondents may form preferences in different ways than actual voters in primaries who possess a much greater array of information about the candidates. If so, we may need to revise these theories of voters' choices that posit a central role for expectations.

3. For the NES's Super Tuesday study, I shall be using only those voters interviewed after the New Hampshire primary. While this decision shrinks the size of the sample, it should provide a better gauge of voters' information. This subset of the total sample is also used in the analyses of the upcoming chapters.

4. One also could compare voters in primaries to voters in midterm congressional elections. This comparison would provide an additional benchmark to judge the information voters in primaries possess. If voters in primaries have less information than participants in midterm elections, that would be much clearer evidence that the former are poorly informed since the latter are generally less informed than those in presidential elections (Mann 1978; Mann and Wolfinger 1980; Jacobson 1987).

I examined this question briefly and found that voters in midterm elections are much less informed than voters in primaries. For instance, about 25 percent of voters in midterm elections knew both candidates' positions on the liberal-conservative spectrum. In January 1980, nearly 75 percent of voters in primaries knew Carter's and Kennedy's positions. These comparisons are only for two-candidate races in primaries. I make this point to show that one's standards will heavily influence the outcome of one's assessment.

5. In 1984, Democratic partisans never gave Jesse Jackson much of a chance to win the nomination. Mondale, on the other hand, was seen by most partisans as the likely nominee, except right after the New Hampshire primary, when Hart edged ahead of Mondale as the most likely Democratic nominee.

6. While "peer review," as Polsby describes it, does not occur in primaries, it is not clear how often party leaders in previous nominating systems made such judgments. Franklin Roosevelt's nomination in 1932, for example, can be largely

attributed to the fact that party leaders thought Roosevelt was capable of winning the general election. Party leaders made little mention of his qualifications for the presidency. For two accounts of the 1932 Democratic nomination see James Farley (1940) and Ralph Martin (1964). While party leaders are clearly more informed than the rank and file, it seems unlikely that "peer review" always occurred in previous systems either, as Polsby himself admits.

═══ 5 ═══

Voting in Presidential Primaries

When assessing the qualifications of voters in primaries to choose presidential candidates, a major issue becomes how these participants form preferences for candidates. While the previous chapter examined the information voters in primaries possess, I have yet to address how they actually go about choosing contenders. This matter is crucial in deciding whether voters in primaries can select good candidates. If voters employ a questionable decision-rule, it becomes problematic as to whether they should be used to select presidential aspirants. But on the other hand, if voters choose candidates in a reasonable fashion, one's faith in using these citizens to select nominees should increase.

Previous research paints a mixed portrait concerning the quality of voters' decisions. Patterson (1980), for instance, argues that the news media play a large role in shaping voters' preferences, which suggests that journalists may be indirectly selecting nominees. Bartels (1988) and Brady and Johnston (1987) lend some support to this view, arguing that the electoral prospects of the candidates play a major role in who voters support. It is, of course, the news media's emphasis on the "horse race" that supplies the information about the chances of the candidates. While Bartels (1988) and Brady and Johnston (1987) contend that "expectations matter," these scholars also find that the candidates' views on issues have some influence on voters' choices. But if their overall findings are correct, it suggests that most voters are swayed primarily by matters that provide few indications about how good a president any of these candidates might make.

Another set of scholars has, however, found that candidates' personal qualities structure the preferences of most voters (Williams et al. 1976;

Gopoian 1982; Norrander 1986b; Abramowitz 1987; Kenney and Rice 1987a). If these studies are correct, then perhaps voters can choose good candidates, since these perceived personal qualities provide at least some insight into their capacities for presidential leadership. On a more troubling note, most of these studies also report that the candidates' views on issues have limited influence on voters' selection of candidates. The failure of issues to guide voters' choices may be seen as a weakness in the way these participants cast their ballots, since some scholars would like to have primaries serve as debates on matters of public policy.

Another source of worry about how voters choose candidates focuses on the great swings in support some aspirants experience during primaries. Hart's rise in 1984 from about 2 percent in the Gallup Poll to over 30 percent in less than two weeks is perhaps the most famous example of this kind of swing. Such shifts suggest that voters may not be making careful assessments of the candidates' abilities for leadership or their views on issues, which questions the quality of those decisions. In addition, these large changes in public opinion seem to support the idea of Bartels and others that expectations may be driving the decisions of voters.

As one can see, there are some reasons to doubt the quality of voters' decisions in primaries. The purpose of this chapter is to sort this matter out. I shall first examine the possible criteria voters use when selecting candidates. I shall then examine the possible causes of the large shifts in voters' preferences for candidates that often occur during the early primaries. This information should shed some light on the quality of voters' decisions.

THE CRITERIA VOTERS IN PRIMARIES USE

There are a number of criteria voters might use when casting ballots in a presidential primary. Among the possibilities are candidates' views on issues, their ideological positions, each candidate's prospect of winning the nomination, and their personal characteristics. In this section I shall examine the likelihood that voters consider each of these criteria when voting in primaries.

Some scholars have suggested that voters may rely on candidates' positions on issues to form preferences. A major reason given is that since primaries are intraparty affairs, partisanship is unlikely to be able to serve as a guide for citizens when voting, forcing them to use other cues such as candidates' views on issues. Steven Brams (1978) makes just such an argument: "Although most of the research that has been conducted [about the primacy of issues] applies to the general election, it would seem even more applicable to primaries, in which party affiliation is not usually a factor" (p. 4). Since the vote in presidential elections is generally determined by issues, candidates, and partisanship, the vote in primaries, the argument goes, should be explained by issues and candidates. This logic leads some scholars to think that issues can be "expected to strongly influence the outcomes of primaries" (Gopoian 1982, p. 525).

While some voters may consider candidates' views on issues when voting, most will probably not. One reason is that in intraparty struggles there are likely to be few significant disagreements about matters of policy between candidates. Many scholars note that there are often few differences between the parties on issues in general elections. This view is exemplified by George Wallace's famous statement that "there is not a dime's worth of difference between the two parties." If there are few differences between parties, there should be even fewer when Democrats face Democrats or Republicans face Republicans, encouraging voters to choose candidates on the basis of other considerations. In 1988, for instance, one commentator argued that Bush and Dole agreed "on virtually all the major issues of the day despite their sometimes rancorous sniping" (Hoffman 1988, p. 13). A second reason that issues are unlikely to play an important role in voters' decisions is that when more than two candidates compete, voters generally do not know each contender's position on the issues (recall the evidence presented in the previous chapter), further discouraging voting on the basis of candidates' views on issues. Finally, even when voters have an idea of candidates' views, their information may not be detailed enough to perceive differences even if they exist.

Many studies that have examined the influence of issues on voting in primaries have turned up little evidence of policy voting (Gopoian, 1982; Marshall 1984; Wattier 1983a; Williams et al. 1976; Norrander 1986b). Relying on the CBS/*New York Times* exit polls for the 1976 presidential primaries, David Gopoian (1982) concludes that "issues generally do not predict the outcomes of the 1976 primaries very well" (p. 523). Bartels (1985) does, however, uncover some support for the contention that voters in primaries consider issues when voting, "particularly in stable contests involving well-known candidates" (p. 812). Brady and Johnston (1987) and more recent work by Bartels (1988) also find that issues matter. But in these studies the amount of issue voting appears small.

Rather than trying to explain the preferences of voters by their perceptions of the candidates' views on issues, I shall conduct a simple three-prong test to see how many voters have a position on a given issue, how many voters know the candidates' positions, and how many voters perceive differences in the candidates' positions.[1] If a voter fails on any one of these three tests, that individual is unlikely to be able to choose candidates on the basis of that issue. While this test will not show how many voters do cast their ballots on the basis of issues, it will

Table 5.1

The Prospects of "Issue" Voting in 1976 (in percent)

	Erie* Republicans	Erie# Democrats	L.A.* Republicans	L.A.@ Democrats	General$ Election
Busing					
+1 to -1	38.4	21.0	45.2	50.3	38.2
0	23.3	9.8	22.0	24.1	23.3
R. DK	0	.7	1.2	.7	1.2
Cand. DK	46.6	70.6	20.8	31.2	24.1
Government Jobs					
+1 to -1	43.7	18.2	37.9	54.6	18.8
0	20.5	7.7	17.1	29.1	8.1
R. DK	2.7	2.1	2.4	1.4	2.6
Cand. DK	37.0	70.6	31.7	27.0	21.3
Abortion					
+1 to -1	23.3	13.2	37.9	29.8	43.9
0	19.2	7.6	24.4	18.4	27.3
R. DK	4.1	3.5	2.4	0	.6
Cand. DK	64.4	77.8	46.3	44.0	23.9
Tax Cut					
+1 to -1	37.0	18.9	45.1	46.2	23.0
0	32.9	10.5	31.7	27.0	10.2
R. DK	0	3.5	1.2	1.4	1.7
Cand. DK	41.1	68.5	30.5	35.4	17.8
Welfare Spending					
+1 to -1	45.2	20.3	46.3	52.4	31.1
0	19.2	8.4	13.4	18.4	14.5
R. DK	0	0	3.7	2.1	.3
Cand. DK	38.4	68.5	17.1	19.8	20.9
Defense Spending					
+1 to -1	38.4	23.8	56.1	53.3	26.8
0	11.0	8.4	24.4	27.7	12.2
R. DK	8.2	2.8	2.4	2.1	3.5
Cand. DK	24.7	66.4	14.6	28.4	15.7

*The data in these columns come from examining voters'
perceptions of Reagan's and Ford' views on issues.
@Voters' perceptions of Jackson and Carter are used to
calculate the proportions in this column.
@The data in this column come from examining voters'
perceptions of Carter's and Brown's views on issues.
$In this column, voters' perceptions of Carter's and Ford's
views on issues are examined.

See Appendix II for the exact wording of questions.

Table 5.1 Continued

```
Symbols in the Table:
"+1 to -1" indicates the proportion of voters who saw the two
candidates within one point of each other on the seven-point
scale.
" 0 " indicates the proportion of voters who saw no difference
between candidates.
"R. DK" indicates the proportion of voters who did not have a
position on the issue.
"Cand. DK" indicates the proportion of voters who did not
know one of the two candidates' positions.

Source: Patterson's 1976 panel study.
```

provide an idea of the likelihood of "issue" voting in primaries. More-over, this procedure will test explicitly the reasons given above for why voting on the basis of issues is unlikely in primaries.

Tables 5.1 and 5.2 show that a large proportion of respondents failed on one or more of these three conditions.[2] In 1980, about 43 percent of voters in Democratic primaries, on average, could not meet the require-ments. The figures were even higher for Democrats and Republicans in the other three contests. In 1976, 58.2 percent of the Democratic elec-torate in Los Angeles could not use defense spending as a criterion for choosing a candidate. Over 80 percent of Democratic voters in Erie typ-ically could not use one of the issues as a criterion to choose a candi-date. This latest figure reflects the fact that most candidates in the pri-mary were not well known to the participants.[3] But even when candidates were well known the prospects for voting on the basis of candidates' views on issues were not great. In contests between Ford and Reagan or Carter and Kennedy, often 25 percent or more of the voters could not identify at least one of the candidates' views on the issue. Moreover, even when they knew the candidates' positions on an issue, they often could not differentiate between them. In the Republican contest in Los Angeles (1976), about 22 percent of the voters, on average, did not see any difference between Reagan and Ford on the six issues listed.

While these data show that many primary voters are unlikely to be able to compare systematically candidates' positions on issues when vot-ing, perhaps they only base their choice on a single issue. Under such circumstances, voters would only need to perceive differences between the candidates on one of the many campaign issues. In the 1980 Demo-cratic contest, about 85 percent of voters could distinguish between Kennedy and Carter on at least one of the five issues. Yet in Erie, only

40 percent of voters in the Democratic primary could discern any difference between Jackson and Carter on even one of the six issues studied. In the 1980 Republican nomination, less than 60 percent of the voters could have used just one of the issues in an effort to choose between Reagan and Bush. These data further indicate that voting on the basis of issues would be difficult for many citizens, especially when one or more of the contenders are not well known.[4]

Perhaps the proportion of voters able to meet the requirements is always low, suggesting that these percentages are misleading. In an effort to test this possibility I examined voters in general elections. Since there are usually greater differences in general elections between the candidates' stances on issues than in primaries, voters in these contests should perceive that—if my reasoning is sound. In addition, this comparison should be of value because issue voting does not seem to dominate the choices of voters in presidential elections. As Richard Niemi and Herbert Weisberg (1984) conclude, "party and candidate factor are the most important" determinants of the vote, "with issues only occasionally being found to play much of a role" (p. 89). Thus, if issue voting is uncommon in the general election, it should be even less common in primaries, providing the differences between the contenders on issues are even less than in the presidential contest.

Tables 5.1 and 5.2 show that typically a higher proportion of voters in general elections met the requirements for voting on the basis of issues. In 1980, for instance, more general-election voters met the requirements than Democratic-primary voters, though the difference was not very large. At times, however, the differences between the two electorates were quite sizable, especially when one examines Erie's voters in the Democratic primary.[5] This last set of data certainly suggests that issue voting is unlikely to be common in primaries.

Keep in mind that these results do not eliminate the possibility that issue voting occurs in primaries. It is likely that issues do play some role, as Bartels (1985, 1988) and others suggest. My point is simply that issues are not likely to be a central criterion of voters when selecting candidates.

Instead of voters knowing the candidates' views on issues, perhaps voters use the ideological orientation of candidates as a way to summarize candidates' views on sets of issues.[6] Anthony Downs (1957) once observed that "a voter finds party ideologies useful because they remove the necessity of his relating every issue to his own philosophy. Ideologies help him focus attention on the differences between parties; therefore they can be used as samples of all differentiating stands. With this short cut a voter can save himself the cost of being informed upon wider range of issues" (p. 98). The idea that ideology could serve as a cost cutter is especially attractive since participants in primaries often

Table 5.2
The Prospects of "Issue" Voting in 1980 (in percent)

	Democrats*	Republicans#	General$ Election
USSR			
+1 to -1	51.0	48.1	26.0
0	25.2	22.2	11.5
R. DK	10.3	9.9	12.2
Cand. DK	12.9	29.6	11.8
Unemployment-Inflation			
+1 to -1	31.4	38.7	20.4
0	11.8	21.2	7.4
R. DK	12.1	28.7	12.8
Cand. DK	25.5	25.1	35.8
Aid to Minorities			
+1 to -1	36.0	55.7	22.1
0	10.0	25.3	7.8
R. DK	8.0	1.3	9.6
Cand. DK	27.0	37.3	14.4
Defense Spending			
+1 to -1	43.1	46.3	20.6
0	13.5	20.0	6.7
R. DK	12.9	8.7	9.7
Cand. DK	10.9	35.0	12.0
Government Services			
+1 to -1	42.4	47.4	23.3
0	16.3	21.2	6.8
R. DK	12.4	16.2	12.7
Cand. DK	8.5	23.7	15.4

*The data in this column come from examining voters'
perceptions of Carter's and Kennedy's views on issues.
#This column of data comes from looking at voters'
perceptions of Reagan's and Bush's views on issues.
$The two candidates used in this column are Carter
and Reagan.

See Table 5.1 for a description of the abbreviations used
in this table. See Appendix II for the exact wording of the
questions used in the table.

Source: The June wave of the 1980 NES panel study and the NES
1980 general election study.

choose between more candidates than do voters in the general election, making voting on the basis of issues difficult, as we saw above. In addition, the campaign in most primaries is usually shorter than that in the general election (except for New Hampshire), making information scarcer and the use of short-cuts even more desirable. A final reason that the ideological stances of the candidates may guide voters' choices is that they could serve as a cue, much like party identification does in the general election (Hedlund 1977–78; Kenney and Rice 1987a).

While there are reasons to think the ideological positions of candidates could shape voters' preferences, some doubts remain. First, Downs referred to "party ideologies" and "differences between parties." Since primaries are *intra*-party struggles, candidates compete, for the most part, on the same portion of the ideological spectrum. The difference in ideological orientation between Ronald Reagan and Walter Mondale was likely to be clearer to voters than that between Gary Hart and Walter Mondale, since the latter two were generally seen as liberals. Thus, voters are likely to perceive fewer ideological differences between most of the candidates in primaries than between candidates in general elections. Second, for the labels to have any meaning, voters must think in ideological terms. Philip Converse (1964), for example, found few voters who could be labeled as ideologues. While much has been written on this subject since Converse (see, for instance, Nie, Verba, and Petrocik 1979; Conover and Feldman 1981), many citizens still do not have a clear grasp of the liberal and conservative labels.[7] Third, candidates often do not stress ideological labels, which would lower the salience of this criterion to voters (Abramowitz 1978).

As with "issue" voting, three conditions must be met for ideological concerns to be important to voters: respondents must have an ideological position, must know the candidates' ideological positions, and must see differences between the ideological positions of the candidates.

The results in Table 5.3 show that a great number of voters could not have used ideological cues when voting in primaries, though the proportion of the electorate meeting these standards varies widely.[8] About 70 percent of the Republican electorate in Los Angeles could use ideological cues, while in Erie only about 30 percent of Democratic voters could use ideology as a cue. This difference reflects the fact that Democratic voters in Erie did not know the candidates as well as the Republicans in Los Angeles did—48.3 percent of Erie voters did not know either Carter's or Jackson's ideological position, compared with only 8.5 percent of Los Angeles voters who did not know either Ford's or Reagan's ideological position. In 1988 about 21 percent of voters could not even rate themselves on the ideological spectrum.[9] Even those voters in primaries who met the minimum requirements for ideological voting often saw very little difference between contenders. In 1988, over a third of the voters interviewed after the New Hampshire primary saw no difference between Bush's and Dole's ideological stances. Among Los Angeles voters in the Republican primary, 51.8 percent saw Reagan and Ford within one point of each other on the seven-point ideological scale.

Table 5.3 also reports on voters in general elections to see if they are able to perceive greater ideological differences between the candidates than voters in primaries. As with "issue" voting, voters in general elections were able to perceive greater ideological differences between the contenders than voters in primaries. This finding further bolsters my claim that ideological voting is not common in primaries or is at least less common than in general elections.

One of the reasons for the absence of perceived ideological differences may be the behavior of candidates. Candidates rarely stress ideological matters when campaigning in primaries, which should lower their saliency to voters. In 1984, Senator Hart, for instance, tried to avoid ideological labels. Initially at least, he was successful; conservatives saw him as conservative while liberals saw him as liberal.[10] Carter similarly avoided ideological labeling in 1976. In James Wooten's words: "He [Carter] is the candidate of a thousand impressions—a liberal, a moderate, a moderate liberal, a conservative moderate, an ambidextrous centrist, a man for all seasons. . . ." Leon Epstein (1978), referring to the 1976 Democratic nomination, observes that "success was not built on anything like the expected left or right modes; insofar as he had an ideological position, it was of the moderate or centrist type that had been thought to suffer under the new order. Nor was Carter the only important Democratic candidate to practice such non-ideological politics. His most formidable late opponent, Governor Brown, was similarly hard to classify in left-right terms" (p. 190).

Ideology need not play a central role in the decisions of voters in primaries. Some observers have thought that ideology is important in primaries because they have seen it as a force similar to that of partisanship in general elections. Hedlund (1977–78), for example, contends that "in a primary election with the absence of many other voting cues and with a wide range of ideological positions represented by the candidates, one might expect ideological differences between voter and candidate to be more salient in the candidate choice" (p. 510). This expectation assumes that voters are presented a clear ideological choice and that voters think along ideological lines. But in fact voters do not see major ideological differences between most candidates and often do not label themselves ideologically.[11]

A third criterion participants in primaries may use when voting involves the electoral chances of the candidates. Recent work on voting in primaries contends that the chances of the contenders greatly influence the choice of voters (Abramowitz 1987; Bartels 1985, 1987, 1988;

Table 5.3
The Prospects of "Ideological" Voting

	R. DK	CAND. DK	NO DIFF.	TOTAL	+1 to -1	N
(In Percent)						
Republicans, Erie 1976	2.7	21.9	20.5	45.1	50.6	73
Democrats, Erie* 1976	7.0	48.3	11.9	67.2	25.9	149
Republicans, L.A. 1976	1.2	8.5	19.5	29.2	51.8	82
Democrats, L.A.* 1976	.7	12.1	31.2	44.0	52.5	141
Republicans, June* 1980	21.2	5.8	12.2	39.2	35.3	83
Democrats, June 1980	19.7	7.9	21.1	48.7	46.1	142
Republicans, Super* Tuesday 1988	10.6	12.5	33.7	56.8	66.4	104
Democrats, Super* Tuesday 1988	22.2	23.1	9.4	54.7	36.8	212
General Election ** 1976	5.5	13.1	8.7	27.3	21.5	344
General Election 1980	27.6	6.4	3.9	37.9	14.0	996
General Election 1984	18.5	7.5	4.5	30.5	13.3	1376

* In the Erie Democratic contest, Carter and Jackson were the two candidates. In Los Angeles, Carter and Brown were the two candidates. In 1980, data for Republican voters involved Bush and Reagan. Jackson and Dukakis were the two contenders for the results from 1988. Bush and Dole filled that role for the Republicans in that year.

** These data are from Patterson's fifth wave.

R. Dk- Respondent does not have an ideological position.
Cand. Dk- Respondent does not know a candidate's
        ideological position.
No Diff.- Respondent sees no difference in ideological
        position between the two candidates.
Total - This proportion is the addition of the percentages
        in the 3 prior columns.

Source: Patterson's 1976 panel study and NES 1980 and 1988 panel and general election studies.

Brady 1984; Brady and Johnston 1987). Bartels (1988), in perhaps the best work to date on voting in primaries, contends that expectations have internalized, direct, and interactive effects on voters' preferences. He finds, for instance, that "Hart gained considerable aggregate support due to the impact of expectations" (p. 128). While Brady and Johnston (1987) offer a slightly different view of how expectations affect voters, they still show that the electability of the candidates shapes the preferences of voters. Abramowitz (1987) also finds some support for the general thesis that expectations matter, writing that "Walter Mondale's comeback after April 3 was due largely to changing perceptions of Mondale's and Hart's chances of winning the nomination and the general election" (p. 50).

There are a number of reasons why expectations may influence the vote.[12] First, voters may simply want to go with a winner. Under this reasoning citizens derive satisfaction from being on a winning team (Bartels 1988, pp. 111–12). The second reason why expectations may shape voters' choices is that these individuals learn primarily about the chances of the candidates from the news media and thus rely on that information to choose candidates. Given the general view that the news media focus on the "horse race," there is some merit in this logic. Third, voters may get caught up in the excitement of the race and jump on a candidate's bandwagon. Bartels (1988) notes that under this reasoning, "momentum looks less like a political process than like a communicable disease. The exposed come down with 'Big Mo' more or less regardless of their political instincts or interests" (p. 111). Finally, voters may only support serious candidates to avoid "wasting" their vote.[13]

While there is good reason to believe that expectations matter, I shall present some data that suggest why such concerns may not figure prominently in the decisions of most voters in primaries. First, many voters do not know the chances of the candidates, and even when they do, the perceptions of the contenders' prospects do not appear to differ enough for them to be able to choose candidates on that basis. For instance, almost one-third of all Democratic partisans shortly after the New Hampshire primary gave Hart and Mondale an equal chance of winning the nomination.[14] In addition, one-quarter of Democratic partisans interviewed between the New Hampshire primary and Super Tuesday did not even know Hart's chances of winning the nomination. In 1976, Udall was still relatively unknown to voters even by the time of the California primary—only 53.9 percent of them were willing to estimate his prospects for victory. Among those who voted for Dole and Bush in 1988, 43 percent had similar assessments of their chances following the New Hampshire primary.[15] Another 10 percent of these voters could not rate either Dole's or Bush's chances for the nomination. On the Democratic side, over 51 percent of those respondents who voted for Gore or Dukakis on Super Tuesday did not know one of the two candidates' electoral prospects. Nearly 13 percent saw little difference between their chances. Even among those who voted for Jackson or Dukakis, over 38 percent could not use the chances of their winning the nomination to sort out the candidates. This proportion is quite high, given the fact that most voters did not see Jackson as a viable contender. Thus, even when there are clear differences in the chances of the candidates, a sizable proportion of voters still could not use that piece of information as a cue.

One could argue that while voters are unlikely to compare the chances of candidates systematically, these strategic concerns could still be important to their decisions. Perhaps voters know only the chances of one or two candidates and use that information to form a preference. While that kind of information can have direct and indirect effects on one's preferences, it seems clear that many voters simply do not support the candidate they perceive as the likely winner. Table 5.4 reports the proportion of respondents who supported the candidate they thought was most likely to win the nomination.[16] In Los Angeles 58.1 percent of voters were incorrectly predicted. In Erie the figure was 32.9 percent. Among Hart and Mondale supporters, 57.3 percent supported the candidate they thought was the most likely to win, while 24.4 percent did not.[17] Similar proportions exist for the 1988 Super Tuesday contests. Evidence from the 1976, 1984, and 1988 campaigns suggests that voters consider more than just the candidates' chances when voting.

As with previous considerations, strategic concerns surely enter the calculations of some voters. The point here is that these matters appear unlikely to dominate the decision-making process of most voters. Voters simply do not appear familiar enough with candidates' chances to use such cues. And even when they are aware of the contenders' prospects, voters appear to see only small differences in the chances of many of the contenders. These findings do not, however, mean that "momentum" does not exist in primaries, but rather that these shifts in support are not due to the strategic assessments of voters in primaries. I shall address this issue in the next section.

The fourth and final consideration involves the personal characteristics of the candidates. This criterion, I contend, is the most important consideration for voters when casting their ballots.[18] The reasons for voters relying primarily on the personal characteristics of the candidates are twofold. First, since primaries often feature large numbers of candidates and since many of these contenders are virtual "unknowns," it is reasonable to suppose that voters rely primarily upon information that is not costly to obtain when making their choices in primaries. One source of readily available and cheaply obtained information concerns the candidates themselves. Both the news media's coverage of the candidates

Table 5.4
Predicting the Vote by the Respondents' Perception of Who Is
Most Likely to Win the Nomination

(In Percent)

	Democrats 1976		Democrats 1984
Predictions	Erie	L.A.	Hart-Mondale
Correct	55.2	33.8	57.3
Error	32.9	58.1	24.4
Null+	11.9	8.1	18.3
N	144t	141	350&

	Democrats 1988	Republicans 1988
Predictions		
Correct	37.8	56.8
Error	33.7	20.0
Null+	28.5	23.2
N	172#	95*

+A null prediction is where the voter rated two or more
candidates equally. These cases yield no prediction.
tThis 'n' includes only voters who voted for Carter, Jackson,
Wallace, or Udall. All other candidates received less than 2
percent of the votes.
&This sample includes only white Democratic identifiers in an
effort to control for the effect of Jackson's candidacy.
#The "n" includes only voters for the top four contenders:
Dukakis, Jackson, Gore and Gephardt. Also note that these
respondents were interviewed after the New Hampshire primary.
*The "n" includes only those who voted for Bush, Dole, Kemp
and Robertson. As with the Democrats, the sample includes only
voters interviewed after the New Hampshire primary.

Source: Patterson 1976 panel study, NES 1984 Continuous Monitoring
study and NES 1988 Super Tuesday study.

and the contenders' own advertising provide two sources of inexpensive
information about the candidates' personal characteristics. This information need not just be in words; it can also be in pictures. Each candidate has a different appearance, speaks differently, and tries to project
a different image. Candidates often stress "leadership" or other personal attributes when campaigning in primaries. In 1984, Mondale stressed
his experience while Hart discussed "new leadership." In 1976, Carter
spent a great deal of time and money stressing his honesty, fairness and
compassion. While the unpaid media often focus on the "winners" and
"losers" of primaries, this coverage still paints images of the candidates
themselves. For instance, after Hart's victory in New Hampshire there

was an upsurge in coverage about him. This coverage pictured him as a confident leader and a "winner." It also talked about his underdog status and how he worked so hard to achieve this victory—information that all reflects positively on Hart's character.[19] Michael Traugott (1985) concurs, arguing that the news media "provided the cues about Hart's success by more and better coverage, most of it highly personalized. He therefore came to be seen as hard working, trustworthy, and competent . . ." (p. 108). This coverage may not be ideal, but it provides information about the personal attributes of the candidates.

A second reason why voters in primaries are likely to rely on the personal characteristics of candidates is that, as shown above, voters often do not know enough detail about the candidates' views on issues, ideological positions, or prospects for victory to vote on the basis of these other concerns. And even if they do possess sufficient information, they often have difficulty perceiving differences between the candidates on these matters.

The best data to estimate the considerations that voters use when casting their ballots come from open-ended questions on why respondents support a given candidate for the nomination since voters can express their reasoning in an unfettered format.[20] In response to these questions, if the voters in primaries cite personal characteristics or the competence of candidates—not candidates' views on issues, ideological orientations, or electoral prospects—as their reasons for voting for the candidate, such a finding would support my claim of the primacy of candidate-centered evaluations.

The percentages in Table 5.5 are the *density* of each type of comment; that is, the proportion of all responses of voters in Erie and Los Angeles that concern issues, ideology, qualities of the candidates, or the campaign. The data show that evaluations of candidates are based largely on personality factors (see Appendix III for coding). The proportion of responses that concern personality is between 62.0 percent and 79.2 percent. The density of comments about issues is about 14 percent. Ideological concerns were rarely mentioned. Concerns about the campaign, which include strategic considerations, varied between .9 percent and 11.0 percent. Concerns about the campaign were most salient in the Democratic contests, probably reflecting the number of contenders in the California and Pennsylvania primaries. Note that the data are from both a two-candidate and a multicandidate contest, suggesting that these findings may be relevant to most presidential primaries. These data are also consistent with evidence presented above showing that voters in primaries were not likely to cast their ballots on the basis of candidates' views on issues, ideological positions, or prospects for victory. In sum, it appears that candidate-centered considerations dominate the reasons

Table 5.5
The Density of the Open-Ended Comments by Voters in
Presidential Primaries

(In Percent)

Reasons for Supporting a Candidate for Nomination

	N	"Personality"	Issues	Ideology	Group	Campaign	Other	DK
Erie Democrats	264	70.1	10.2	.8	9.5	8.7	.4	.4
Erie Republicans	101	79.2	15.8	2.0	0	2.0	1.0	0
LA Democrats	270	68.9	15.9	5.2	1.9	7.8	.4	0
LA Republicans	161	73.9	19.9	3.1	0	1.2	1.9	0

Reasons for Voting for Candidates

	N	"Personality"	Issues	Ideology	Group	Campaign	Other	DK
Erie Democrats	281	62.6	14.9	1.4	8.2	11.0	1.1	.7
Erie Republicans	108	62.0	5.6	1.9	.9	.9	28.7	0
LA Democrats	278	72.7	12.6	2.8	2.2	6.5	3.2	0
LA Republicans	147	76.8	13.6	5.4	.6	2.0	1.4	0

See Appendix III for coding scheme and the wording of the
questions.
N refers to the number of comments, not the number of
respondents.

Source: Patterson's 1976 panel study.

voters cite for supporting the candidates, though, at times, issues and
strategic considerations constitute a significant portion of the concerns.[21]
One might argue, however, that data from open-ended questions encourage "personality" responses since they focus attention directly on
the candidates. If so, then these data are not particularly useful. The
general-election NES surveys provide a way to test for this possibility
because they ask what respondents like or dislike about each of the ma-

jor candidates. While the question wording and the population of the samples are different, the format of the questions is similar. The comparison is useful because both questions allow the voter to state whatever is on his or her mind. If voters in general elections cite "personality" concerns as often as voters in primaries, then perhaps it is the format of the question that encourages these types of responses, not that voters in primaries are likely to consider these matters when voting.

The proportion of candidate-centered comments is, however, dramatically lower in general elections: 23.3 percent of all comments in 1980, 31.2 percent in 1976, and 33.9 percent in 1972.[22] These figures are about 40 percent lower than those found among Erie and Los Angeles primary voters. The comparison is not exact, but the magnitude of the difference suggests that voters in primaries focus more on the candidates' personal characteristics than do general-election voters.

The evidence presented so far is consistent with the notion that the candidates' personal style and leadership are the major criteria voters use when selecting candidates. But works by Gregory Markus and Philip Converse (1979) and Benjamin Page and Calvin Jones (1979) show that the determinants of the vote are locked in a causal web. That is, these various criteria are related simultaneously to each other. Thus, to be sure of my findings, one needs to take account of such interactions. In an important piece of work, Kenney and Rice (1987a) develop just such a model, using measures of ideology, issues, expectations, and the personal qualities of the candidates to explain the preferences of Democratic and Republican identifiers in June 1980. After estimating this simultaneous model, they report that the qualities of the candidates "were the strongest direct determinant of nomination preference" (p. 15). The personal characteristics of the candidates also had an indirect influence, shaping the respondents' perception of the candidates' ideological positions and views on issues. They did find, like Bartels and others, that issues, ideology, and expectations also influence the decisions of voters. But as my results above suggest, the dominant criterion of voters in primaries is the personal characteristics of the contenders.

MOMENTUM IN PRESIDENTIAL PRIMARIES

One of the most interesting aspects of voting in primaries is the often large swings in support for the candidates. For instance, Gary Hart gained 30 percentage points in his Gallup poll rating in a matter of days. What caused this rapid shift in support? Some scholars, as suggested above, contend that voters are responding, in large part, to the changing chances of the candidates (Patterson 1980; Brady 1984; Bartels 1985, 1987, 1988). Given the evidence presented above and in Chapter 4, it is unlikely voters respond in such a strategic matter. Voters simply do not have sufficient information to act in that way. In this section I shall attempt to explain these large shifts in support and by so doing provide additional insight into how voters choose candidates.

In primaries, many voters prior to casting their ballots are uncommitted to any of the candidates or have a weak preference for one of the candidates. Ample evidence exists to support this claim. For example, according to a 1984 CBS/*New York Times* poll, 50 percent of self-identified Democrats changed their preferences during the campaign for the nomination.[23] Among Republican voters in 1988 who supported a particular candidate in the preelection wave, 37 percent altered their preferences following Super Tuesday. Bush's rapid fall after his Iowa win in 1980 is another case in point. He appeared to have "momentum" and support going into New Hampshire. Immediately following his success in Iowa, 45 percent of the Republicans in New Hampshire supported him.[24] But Reagan was able to puncture Bush's paper-thin support. Bush received only 22.7 percent of the vote in New Hampshire, suggesting that at least 20 percent of the electorate had very weak preferences. Similar patterns surfaced in 1972, 1976 and 1988. In 1976, Carter rose from obscurity (0.7 percent) in January to 29.3 percent by March 16th. In January 1988, Dukakis had the support of 8 percent of registered voters in the South. A month later, a quarter of that electorate preferred the governor of Massachusetts. McGovern's Gallup poll rating was 5 percent in March; by the middle of April his support was 17 percent, and it continued to rise until by June, 30 percent of Democrats supported his nomination. While some of the cases are not as dramatic as others, they all suggest that many voters are not strongly committed to particular candidates.

It is, I shall argue, the large number of weakly committed voters that generates the often rapid shifts in support for candidates. These voters probably ride a "bandwagon" during presidential primaries. But instead of responding directly to the chances of candidates as some theories suggest, weakly committed voters respond to the flow of positive attention by the news media accorded the "winners" of the early contests. Patterson (1980) shows how the news coverage heavily favors the "winners" of primaries. The attention these candidates receive in the news media is likely to be positive, while the losers may receive negative coverage or perhaps no coverage at all. Following the 1984 New Hampshire primary, for instance, Hart was shown speaking before cheering crowds and talking to reporters of success rather than explaining failure—as Mondale and Glenn were doing. Dan Rather in his coverage of the New Hampshire primary introduced a segment about Hart by stating "earlier tonight, a *confident* Gary Hart, *joy and exuberance* dancing in his eyes, came to our New Hampshire headquarters. This self-proclaimed Democrat of new ideas, the soul of the new machine, talked about his victory over Walter Mondale in New Hampshire."[25] With this kind of upbeat coverage, many weakly committed voters may form a positive, though weak, impression of the candidate.

Hart's rapid rise in the polls in 1984 clearly did not occur because he was viewed as the favorite for the Democratic nomination. Prior to New Hampshire, Mondale was overwhelmingly seen as the likely nominee by partisans nationally.[26] Moreover, *only* 25 percent of Hart's voters in New Hampshire actually thought he would win the nomination.[27] These data suggest that Hart's jump in support, at least initially, cannot be attributed simply to the fact that voters thought he was a likely Democratic nominee. Instead, Hart began to receive a lot of attention after the Iowa caucuses.[28] A large number of potential New Hampshire voters were probably not excited about Mondale, and there was a new candidate—he was young, had a fresh face, and boasted of "new ideas."[29] So a large proportion of the New Hampshire electorate voted for Hart. If Hart had not received the positive attention by the news media he would probably not have soared to his New Hampshire win (Moore 1984a). Roger Mudd of NBC offered a similar assessment of Hart's rise when reporting on the evening of the New Hampshire primary: "Hart can no longer walk down a Manchester street alone. The media won't let him. The day after Iowa the Hart campaign became a media phenomenon. And with only a week between Iowa and New Hampshire, there hasn't been time for questions, only impressions. Hart himself has been skilled, picturing Mondale as something out of the nineteenth century, emphasizing what he calls his new generation of leadership . . . ."[30]

The crucial component of this bandwagon scenario is that most voters have little information about the candidates. When voters have little or no information, any new information will create images about the candidates. Given the positive coverage that follows a winner, this initial impression of the candidate is likely to be favorable. Donald Matthews (1978) describes Carter's 1976 success in similar terms: "There was little Hubert Humphrey or Henry Jackson could do to alter their public images. But Carter's unfamiliarity allowed him to convey a fresh approach to politics, stressing personal qualities—trustworthiness, morality, compassion, technical ability, efficiency, love, practicality" (p. 69). Of course, the reverse can also be true: if a relatively unknown candidate begins to receive bad press, voters may start to respond less positively to that contender.[31]

Bandwagons of this kind, therefore, are unlikely to occur in races where the competing candidates are generally well known, such as the Ford-Reagan and the Carter-Kennedy battles (Patterson 1980, p. 126). When voters know the candidates, they will generally have stronger preferences and more information about the candidates, making large shifts in loyalties less likely. Of course, the news media's coverage will have some influence in races featuring well-known candidates since some voters will have weak preferences or no preferences at all. My point, however, is that there are not enough uncommitted or weakly committed voters to generate large shifts in the support of the candidates.

Another way to think about this argument is that voters rely on two major sources of information when choosing candidates: prior knowledge of the candidates and what they have learned through the media.[32] With well-known candidates competing, prior information plays an important role in shaping preferences. When voters cannot rely on such previous information, they turn to information available in newspapers, on radio, or on television. And if the information the news media provide heavily favors one candidate and voters have little prior information about that candidate, previously weakly committed voters are more likely to cast their ballots for the "favored" contender.

What evidence supports my particular view of bandwagon voting? First, as shown above, voters consider the personal characteristics of the candidates. If voters were citing strategic concerns, then my theory would be suspect; instead it appears that the information voters receive creates impressions about the candidates' personalities. Moreover, as we shall see in Chapter 6, voters *do* receive a good deal of substantive information from the news media coverage of the campaign, making it more likely that voters can weigh the personal characteristics of the candidates when voting.

Second, if my reasoning is correct, only relatively unknown candidates should have benefited from a bandwagon effect. In national nominating conventions, both front-runners and dark horses have ridden a sudden wave of support, but in fact only relative unknowns have ridden bandwagons in primaries: Bush in 1980, Carter in 1976, Hart, and McGovern.[33] Figures 5.1 and 5.2 clearly demonstrate this point.[34] Under the traditional idea of bandwagon voting, the key variable is the chance of the candidate, not whether the candidate is well known or not. Yet in primaries the latter appears to be an important requirement.

Third, as the campaign for the nomination progresses, there should be fewer significant shifts, since voters will begin to accumulate more information and form more stable assessments of the candidates. In addition, the initial one-sided coverage by the press of the "favored" candidate will end as the news media become more critical. In Hart's case, for instance, the news media started to question whether he had "new ideas" and to focus on why he lied about his age and had changed his name. The data support this hypothesis. While some large shifts still occur late in the season, there are fewer of them and they are often smaller than the earlier changes in support (see Figures 5.1 and 5.2).

Fourth, positive coverage of an unknown candidate in the press should result in an increase in the popularity of that aspirant. Patterson (1980)

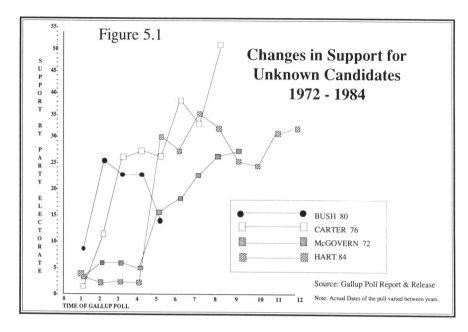

in his study of the 1976 primaries came to just that conclusion: "Initially news messages about Carter's style, which dominated early coverage of him, were extremely favorable—from the opening primary until the final moment of the convention, there were more than two favorable news

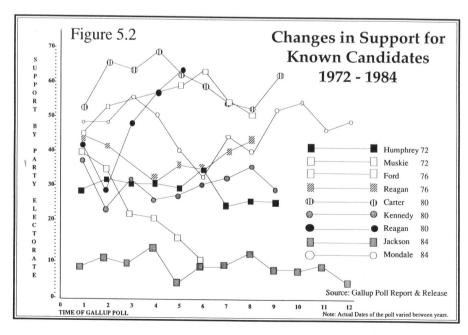

messages about Carter for each unfavorable one. Correspondingly, Carter's early image was extremely positive" (p. 139).

In sum, voters are likely to ride on the "media bandwagon" if they are largely unfamiliar with one of the contending candidates prior to the prenomination campaign. Voters, however, may not be responding directly to the news media's strategic assessments of the candidates but rather to the favorable or unfavorable information provided about the candidates. Thus, while in a sense voters act strategically, it is the media that are the real strategic actors in this nomination game.

CONCLUSION

The results of this chapter shed additional light on the qualifications of voters to choose presidential nominees. While some voters may vote for candidates on the basis of the contenders' positions on issues, their ideological stance, or their chances of winning, most voters rely on the perceived personal characteristics of the candidates as the major consideration when voting. The use of this criterion is quite defensible. Donald Kinder and Robert Abelson (1981) provide one line of defense, arguing that "candidates must appear to be up to the demands of the Presidency. They must invite the public's trust. They must provoke pride, hope and sympathy. And they must steer clear of decisions and activities that earn the public's anger, disgust, fear or unease." Even the Founding Fathers felt that presidents should be selected "for their character, experience and virtue . . ." (Heale 1982, p. 13).

An additional reason why this criterion is defensible is that in an intraparty struggle there are unlikely to be major policy debates because members are likely to agree on many of the important issues. While, of course, there will be some disagreement among the candidates over matters of policy, the amount of disagreement will often be small.[35] The debate instead centers on who is to lead the party, inevitably involving the candidates themselves. Perhaps, then, voters in primaries should choose between leaders rather than ideologies or issues.

While the criterion most voters employ when selecting nominees is reasonable, this chapter has revealed a number of weaknesses about how voters choose candidates. First, at the outset of the campaign many voters have weak preferences, making them susceptible to any new information presented to them, especially from the news media. This weakness has serious implications because it appears that voters may be least able to choose candidates wisely in the early primaries, yet it is at this point where many of the important decisions are made about who will win the nomination.

Another criticism of the way voters choose candidates is that they often are not well acquainted with all the contending candidates. This point was made in the previous chapter and reinforced in this chapter when many voters appeared unable to pick candidates on the basis of their views on issues, ideological positions, or chance for victory. Being unfamiliar with these matters is not as serious a problem as previously thought since it is reasonable for voters to cast their ballots on the basis of personality concerns. It is not clear, however, whether voters have good information about candidates' personal attributes, especially in the early contests. But as the primary season progresses, voters appear to become more informed about the contenders (Patterson 1980; Brady and Johnston 1987; Bartels 1988). Moreover, voters do seem to be generally familiar with the "serious" contenders even at the outset of the campaigns. These two "facts" suggest that under some, but clearly not under all conditions, voters in primaries may be able to choose candidates well.

The final criticism involves the news media's role in the voters' choice of candidates. Many of the weaknesses of voters' decision-making appear to be linked to the central role the news media play in supplying information to voters. The question becomes, then, whether the news media's influence is destructive or constructive. It is to this question I now turn.

NOTES

1. Campbell et al. (1960) posited a similar test for "issue voting," arguing that there were three prerequisites for it to occur: a voter must have an opinion about a given issue, the issue should be salient to the voter, and the voter must think that one of the candidates better represents his or her position than do other candidates (p. 170). Because saliency is a condition I cannot measure with my data, I have to assume that either the questions used are salient to the voters or that they compose a representative sample of issues in the primaries and thus provide some idea of the perceived differences concerning issues. The issues cover a broad range of topics from abortion to military spending to economic concerns. This breadth makes it likely that many voters would find at least some of these issues relevant to their choice of candidates.

2. Table 5.1 reports only the comparison between Jackson and Carter—the two main contenders in Pennsylvania—and Carter and Brown—the two main contenders in California. One might contend that these candidates are not representative of the differences in issues that the complete field of candidates had to offer. If one treats Wallace and Bayh as the two contenders, few voters, as one might expect, see these candidates agreeing on many issues. But about 75 percent of respondents did not know either Wallace's or Bayh's positions on any of the six issues, making issue voting unlikely. The same is true for using Wallace and Morris Udall as the two major contenders. These questions are on a seven-point scale. For the actual wording of the questions see Appendix II.

3. The figures present in Tables 5.1 and 5.2 treat each primary as a two-candidate race. Issue voting in primaries, under my definition, would be even

less likely in contests of three or more candidates. The conditions for issue voting in a three-candidate race are even harder than in a two-candidate race because the voter would need to know the positions of three candidates and perceive differences between all three. As the number of candidates increases the information demands of issue voting are more difficult, and hence fewer voters meet the criteria. Consequently, my data *underestimate* the potential for issue voting in contests of three or more candidates.

4. These data suggest that issue voting may be more likely in contests with well-known candidates—evidence that is consistent with Bartels's (1985) argument.

5. This last bit of evidence does not, of course, indicate how much voting on the basis of issues goes on in primaries. But one can at least conclude that the likelihood of ''issue'' voting in primaries is less than in general elections.

6. Pamela Conover and Stanley Feldman (1981) contend that ideological labels are symbolic rather than based on issues. Even so, ideological labels would still provide voting cues.

7. Teresa Levitin and Miller (1979) write, however, that although people do not seem to understand ideological labels, ''ideological location is an important factor in shaping voters' choices on election day'' (p. 769). Their argument applies, of course, to the general election. In presidential primaries it may have less relevance because intraparty struggles are likely to have fewer ideological differences than in the general election, making it even harder for voters to employ this cue.

8. The data on the likelihood of ideological voting are from the closed-ended questions, which ask respondents to identify their own ideological positions and that of candidates.

9. The proportions of voters cited from the 1988 NES Super Tuesday study refer only to voters surveyed *after* the New Hampshire primary. The reason for using this specific set of voters is that voters in these primaries were more likely to pay attention to the candidates after New Hampshire. The data in Chapter 4 support this point. Note that all future proportions cited from the 1988 study rely on this subset of voters.

10. A March 1984 CBS/*New York Times* poll asked Democrats to characterize themselves and Gary Hart on a liberal-conservative scale. The findings were that respondents ''were likely to place him where they placed themselves.'' *New York Times*, March 29th, 1984, Section D, p. 6.

11. Wattier (1983b) uses ideology to try to account for voters' decisions in Republican primaries. Wattier uncovers a high correlation between the ideological proximity of candidates to the respondent and the respondent's vote: ''The correlation (gamma) between ideological proximity and the vote is .72, .81, .53 and .77 for Florida, Illinois, Massachusetts and New Hampshire, respectively.'' Wattier notes, however, that the correlations may be due to projection rather than any causal connection (p. 1124).

Moreover, the surveys Wattier relies on do not provide information on the number of respondents who do not think in ideological terms (i.e., the ''don't knows''). Converse (1974) suggests that the absence of the ''don't know'' category forces the respondent to give an attitude when he or she has none. This problem would further complicate Wattier's results.

12. Bartels (1988) provides a very useful discussion on expectations and the vote in primaries.

13. In primaries, another type of voting that involves strategic considerations also has been posited: "party voting." Party voting is "where a primary voter chooses the most electable candidate even if the candidate is not the voter's first choice" (Brady 1984). This type of voting is unlikely to be frequent because many voters will be uncertain about the eventual nominee's opponent in the general election, which would discourage "party voting" (Brady, 1984). In addition, the primaries themselves may be taken by voters as indications of a candidate's chances to win the general election. An accurate assessment of any candidate's chances, then, may involve how he or she did in each primary. Yet when voting in the early or middle primaries voters, obviously, do not know the outcome of future contests. This confounding effect further adds to the voter's uncertainty.

14. Note that the data for 1984 are Democratic partisans, not voters in primaries. While I prefer using only data about voters (recall the findings in Chapter 4), the 1984 battle for the nomination is an important one when looking at the role of expectations. Thus, I included some analyses from the 1984 NES Continuous Monitoring Study.

15. By *similar* I mean that respondents rated Dole and Bush within the same range. That is, I recoded the chances of the candidates to a five point scale: 0–24 = 1, 25–49 = 2, 50 = 3, 51–75 = 4, and 76–100 = 5. So if a respondent rated Dole as having a 53 percent chance of winning and Bush a 68 percent chance of winning, I rated them "similar." This scheme is used for the remaining proportions in the text's paragraph.

One might have quarrels with this particular scale, arguing that I should have used a 10-point scale or perhaps even left the data in their original form. Obviously other scales could have been used, but I think my system is at least a reasonable one. First, most voters clearly do not use the 100-point scale. Most estimates clump around certain intervals, such as 50, suggesting that recoding does not involve a loss of much information. Second, it is not clear that voters understand these probabilities. For instance, if you add up the respondents' estimates of each candidate's chances, they often total up to way over 100 percent. So when a voter rates one candidate at 60 percent and another at 65 percent, it is not clear what if any difference exists.

16. One might argue that projection biases these data and thus that they are not good estimates of the candidates' real chances. Instead the responses are proxies for which candidates they like and dislike. Perhaps so, but any bias would make the accuracy artificially high. Thus if the predictive accuracy is low, that still confirms my argument that strategic calculations are not central to voters' decisions.

17. While the 1984 results point to a greater potential for bandwagon voting than in 1976, attitudes toward the candidates themselves (as measured by "feeling" thermometers) were better predictors of the vote than the chances of the candidates.

18. Williams et al. (1976) arrive at a conclusion similar to mine in examining the 1972 New Hampshire presidential primary. They state that "the role of personal characteristics, as perceived by the electorate, appeared to be an impor-

tant factor in decisionmaking in this primary election . . ." (p. 47). Marshall (1984) reaches similar conclusions about the 1980 primaries.

19. Evidence is from a videotape of NBC and CBS news specials following the New Hampshire primary.

20. Since the open-ended format allows respondents to state what is on their minds, respondents should cite concerns that are salient to them. See Kelley (1983) for a useful discussion of the advantages of such data. Most surveys on primaries do not use the open-ended format, making such data scarce. In the Patterson panel, however, there are two sets of open-ended questions.

21. Marshall (1983), using similar data, arrives at the same conclusion about the 1980 campaign, arguing that "the candidates' personal qualities are a significant factor in explaining polls during the presidential nominations race" (p. 656).

22. The NES groups the open-ended responses into broad topics, such as candidates' experience, leadership qualities, and personal characteristics. These are the types of comments I treated as "candidate-centered." In 1980, for example, the codes ran from 0201 to 0498.

23. See *New York Times*, March 27th, 1984, section B, p. 6.

24. The data were presented in the *New York Times*, March 2nd, 1980, section A, p. 16.

25. This passage comes from CBS News's special report on the New Hampshire primary (my emphasis).

26. Mondale was seen by 64 percent of the partisans as having greater than a 50 percent chance of winning the nomination. Glenn was the closest with 30 percent of partisans giving him at least a 50 percent shot at heading the ticket in November.

27. These data are from NBC News's exit poll for New Hampshire.

28. This attention reflected the news media's view that Hart was the alternative to Mondale since he finished second in the Iowa caucuses. Moore (1984b) makes a similar argument.

29. Bartels (1987) offers up a similar description of the 1984 Democratic nomination.

30. This quote is from the NBC Evening News on the day of the New Hampshire primary.

31. Bartels (1985) reaches a similar conclusion: "it appears that supporters flock to the candidate with momentum mostly because he is new, exciting, and getting a lot of attention, and that they bolster this diffuse support with more specific, reasoned political judgments only later (or, if the candidate fades, not at all)" (p. 812). While Bartels's argument has much in common with mine, he argues that "expectations" strongly shape the preferences of voters. I contend, in contrast, that "expectations" do not directly influence the preferences of most voters. Instead, the news media have "expectations" that shape their coverage of the candidates and the voters in turn respond to this coverage in instances where the candidate is largely unknown.

32. The media, in this case, actually involve both the "paid" and "unpaid" media.

33. Reagan's support in 1980 appeared to be rising continuously after January, which implies a possible bandwagon for a well-known candidate. By early March, however, Reagan had no real competition for the nomination and thus gained

support by default. The same was true for Bush in 1988. In fact, one should expect momentum to occur in primaries by default. That is, as candidates fade from the scene their supporters will adopt new preferences. Thus, the winnowing process, by definition, forces the remaining candidates to gain strength.

34. For instance, when comparing the average slopes in Figures 5.1 and 5.2, they are much steeper for unknown candidates (3.5) than for known candidates (.89). Similar data for 1988 are unavailable. Gallup did only a handful of national surveys, instead focusing on specific states and the regions involving the Super Tuesday contests.

35. For instance, in the 1984 Democratic struggle the debate over the nuclear freeze generally involved the question of who was the *first* to support it. This "disagreement" is reflected in both the debates between Mondale and Hart and their own paid advertising.

6

The Media and Voters in Presidential Primaries

A common concern of scholars when assessing the current nominating system involves the news media's influence on voters in presidential primaries.[1] The general view is that since voters in primaries are not well informed about the candidates, they become dependent on the news media's treatment of the contenders when making decisions. Gary Orren and Nelson Polsby (1987), for instance, suggest that because voters in primaries have less information about candidates than their counterparts in the general election, they "are more susceptible . . . to the stories the media choose to emphasize in their news coverage" (p. 4). F. Christopher Arterton (1984) echoes a similar concern, arguing that the news media's coverage of contenders "may indirectly suggest to voters which candidates they should consider supporting" (p. 7). The rapid rise (or fall) of contenders like McGovern, Carter, Bush, and Hart seems to offer support for these assessments.

This perceived influence has led some scholars to suggest that journalists, not voters in primaries, may be "the true arbiters of the nominating process" (Ceasar 1982, p. 60).[2] The purpose of this chapter is to assess the influence the news media have on voters in primaries. There is, of course, no doubt that the news media are central actors in this process. It is not clear, however, that this influence is as pervasive as some suggest. For instance, one can bemoan the fact that Hart was able to win the New Hampshire Primary in 1984 after having at best a modest showing in Iowa. And clearly the news media's coverage of him after Iowa contributed heavily to his rise in the polls (Moore 1984a; Brady and Johnston 1987). But the rise that Hart (or anyone else who might have done unexpectedly well) experienced was also attributable to Mondale's soft support in the electorate. Note that Dole and Gephardt in 1988 and Bush in 1980 did well in Iowa yet lost in New Hampshire. The reason may be that Reagan in 1980, Bush in 1988, and Dukakis in 1988 had strong enough support in that state to withstand any "boost" the winners of the Iowa caucuses might receive. These cases are hardly conclusive, but they suggest that we may be overstating the influence of the news media on the selection process.

It is beyond the scope of the present chapter to decide who are the "true" arbiters of the current nominating arrangement, the voters or the media. The answer surely lies somewhere in between: both voters and journalists play a critical role in the choice of a nominee. Rather than trying to sort out this thorny issue, this chapter will focus on more limited though nonetheless important concerns. Specifically, it shall address two complaints about the news media's influence on voters, both involving the way they supply information to the public. First, many critics question the news media's "excessive" reporting of the "horse race" since it may prevent voters from making judgments about candidates on the basis of more substantive concerns (Patterson 1980; Marshall 1981; Weaver et al. 1981). Second, critics contend that the news media's decisions about which candidates are "serious" shape voters' preferences for candidates, thus preventing them from considering the full range of choices available to them (Ceasar 1982; Crotty and Jackson 1985; Matthews 1978).

THE HORSE RACE

Many scholars question the "excessive" reporting of the horse race during the string of primaries that run from February to June (see, for instance, Patterson 1980; Marshall 1981). There is little doubt that the news media focus on the "game aspect" when covering primaries. One need only listen to the evening news or read a newspaper following a presidential primary. For instance, the *New York Times* printed the following headline the morning after the 1980 New Hampshire primary:

REAGAN EASILY DEFEATS BUSH
AND BAKER IN NEW HAMPSHIRE;
CARTER VICTOR OVER KENNEDY

In general, about 80 percent of the headlines in the *New York Times* front page from 1972 to 1988 focused on the game aspect of the nomination contests (see Table 6.1). In Patterson's (1980) examination of the 1976 newspaper coverage of primaries in Erie and Los Angeles, more than twice as many stories focused on the "game" rather than on something substantive about the candidates. Michael Robinson and Margaret

Table 6.1
The Number of Front-Page Stories About the Battle for the
Nomination

	Number of Stories	Percent Concerning the "Game"
1952 Republicans	75	87%
1952 Democrats	43	87%
1956 Democrats	61	66%
1960 Democrats	63	86%
1964 Republicans	51	88%
1968 Republicans	42	81%
1968 Democrats	73	90%
1972 Democrats	76	83%
1976 Republicans	51	75%
1976 Democrats	101	82%
1980 Republicans	42	83%
1980 Democrats	42	83%
1984 Democrats	86	81%
1988 Republicans	32	80%
1988 Democrats	41	78%

These data are from the New York Times front page. For each
year, the data were collected from January 1st of the election
year to the last primary in June. This analysis concerns only
the headlines of the stories, not the content of the articles
themselves.

Source: Compiled by author.

Sheenan (1983) and Brady and Johnston (1987) find the same pattern for
1980 and 1984, respectively.

Many scholars find this type of coverage troubling because voters may
not be getting the kind of information necessary to make good choices.
As Patterson (1980) argues: "casual daily news exposure does not produce informed voters. It results only in a partial awareness of those sub-
jects that repeatedly appear at the top of the news. Voters consequently
are more conversant about candidates' campaign styles and successes
than about their platforms and leadership skills" (p. 174). Crotty and
Jackson (1985) concur, arguing that the "information transmitted by
television . . . tends to be superficial, based on image more than substance" (p. 75). Brady and Johnston (1987) take a slightly different tack,
arguing that the "real problem with primaries is not that citizens do not
eventually learn about the candidates. Rather, they learn too slowly about
every aspect of the candidates except their viability" (p. 184).

If voters learn primarily about the "game" aspect, it may affect the criteria they use to choose a candidate. So instead of weighing the candidates' views on issues or their ability to lead, voters cast their ballots on the basis of the media's assessment of the candidates' viability (see, for instance, Bartels 1988). This concern is especially worrisome when less well known candidates compete in primaries since voters acquire much of their information about them from the news media. For these contenders, voters may respond primarily to the news media's horse-race coverage, not any assessments of their qualifications for office.

This problem may not, however, be as serious as some scholars suggest because the distinction between "game" and "substance" is less clear cut than is often thought. Critics seem to assume that by focusing on who wins and loses, the news media do not provide insights about the candidates themselves. This assumption is false. While the headlines describe who won and who lost, the follow-up coverage often provides information about the candidates. This coverage might concern the issues the contenders stressed, their personalities, campaign tactics, or gaffes. Consider John Chancellor's comments following the 1988 New Hampshire primary:

Among the political goodies picked up by George Bush yesterday is one important fact. In New Hampshire, at least, Bush wasn't hurt by the Iran-Contra scandals. In our poll of voters, only one in five said the scandals were an important factor in how they voted. I was one of those who thought Iran-Contra might hurt the Vice President. And I now eat my words, probably not a bad thing for a commentator to do once in a while.

But the five words spoken last night by Bob Dole will be harder for him to swallow. Dole to Bush: "Stop lying about my record." That nasty crack instantly became part of the folklore of this campaign. And it was a stunning example of Bob Dole's greatest weakness: that he has a mean streak.[3]

These kinds of assessments provide some clues about the candidates. In this particular case, Chancellor is commenting on a personality trait of Robert Dole. The information may not be ideal, but knowing the temperament of presidential contenders is relevant to voters' choices.

More systematic evidence can be found in the recent work by Brady and Johnston (1987). Their research points to the difficulty of distinguishing simply between "game" and "substance." They develop six categories of news coverage: (1) the potential success of the candidates, (2) their sources of support, (3) their personal characteristics, (4) their views on issues, (5) what they say about each other, and (6) "other" events in the campaign. It seems that two of the six categories fit the idea of substance: coverage of the candidates' views on issues and their personal characteristics. Clearly, discussion by the news media of the candidates' potential for success falls in line with the horse race. The other three categories highlight the difficulty of distinguishing between "game" and "substance." For instance, what candidates say about each other may involve elements of the horse race or it could be an effort by one contender to cast doubt about an opponent's qualifications—clearly a more "substantive" matter. The same is true for coverage about sources of the candidate's support. On the one hand, such reporting may focus on matters relevant to a candidate's prospects for victory. On the other hand, an endorsement by a particular group may aid voters in sorting out a contender's views on issues.

Using Brady and Johnston's (1987) data, one gets a different assessment of the possible role of the horse race in the media's coverage of the campaign. For instance, in 1984, 37.4 percent of the stories by UPI focused on either the candidates themselves or their views on issues. About 25 percent of the stories dealt with the game aspect. The remaining 37.7 percent fell in the gray area: sources of support (9.6 percent), comments about other candidates (9.3 percent), and events in the campaign (18.8 percent).[4] How one catalogs these other stories greatly influences one's perception of the amount of horse-race coverage. I am not advocating any specific scheme. Rather, my point is that the distinction between "game" and "substance" may not be as clear as many scholars assume. And, if so, voters may be receiving better information than many critics suggest.

An additional reason to doubt that the heavy focus on the "game" prevents voters from acquiring substantive information is provided by Robinson and Sheehan (1983). They argue that the horse race provides a "sugar coating" that allows voters to "swallow" the more substantive information (p. 151). Thus, the game aspect may ironically provide a way for voters to learn more about candidates' personalities and their views on some issues than they would without it.

There are also reasons to believe that the news media's coverage of the horse race does not adversely affect the criteria voters in primaries employ when choosing candidates. While these participants may be subjected to who are the winners and losers, they still appear to weigh substantive concerns when voting. As shown in Chapter 5, voters primarily consider the personal characteristics of candidates and to a lesser extent their views on issues when casting their ballots. In fact, as noted in the previous chapter, when all possible criteria are considered in a simultaneous equation, strategic matters play only a marginal role in the calculations of voters (Kenney and Rice 1987a). So even if the news media spend too much time on the strategic aspect of the campaign, they do not appear to prevent voters from making judgments on the basis of substantive concerns.

One must also remember that the news media's focus on the game aspect is part of all elections (Graber 1971, 1972, 1989; Robinson and

Sheehan 1983), not just presidential primaries. Thomas Patterson and Robert McClure (1976) argue, for instance, that in the 1972 presidential election "about nine times as many minutes were given to campaign activity as to the analysis of the candidates' qualifications on key personal and leadership traits and almost four times as many minutes were given to the candidates' positions on the election's critical issues" (p. 41). Such coverage of general elections does not prevent voters from making substantive evaluations of the presidential nominees. Numerous studies document that voters judge candidates on the basis of their views on issues, ideological positions, party affiliations, and personality traits (see, for instance, Kelley 1983). If the news media's coverage of the game aspect does not prevent voters in general elections from making choices on the basis of substantive information about the candidates, it need not do so for their counterparts in primaries.[5]

Another reason to believe voters can cast their ballots on the basis of more substantive criteria is that the news media do not have a monopoly on voters' information. One additional source of information is the paid advertising of the contenders. Patterson and McClure (1976) have documented that paid advertisement "of a presidential candidate contains a fair amount of information on a variety of issues . . ." (p. 122). One, of course, could argue that voters do not pay attention to the paid advertisements of the candidates, and thus this information is of little value. Voters in primaries may, however, be more likely to pay attention to these advertisements than voters in general elections because they may have little information about many of the contenders, and these 30-second spots provide an inexpensive source of it.[6]

A collection of advertisements from presidential primaries in 1984 and 1988 indicates that about 97 percent dealt with either some issue in the campaign or the personalities of the candidates. Often the difference between "issue" and "personality" was not clear, but the advertisements did not deal with the game aspect of the contest. Only 1 of the 34 advertisements examined even talked about the strategic elements of the campaign.[7] In that one particular case, Hart argued that if Mondale won the nomination, Reagan would be able to rerun the 1980 election by tying the former vice-president to the failed presidency of Jimmy Carter. But even in this spot substantive topics were mentioned.

Some observers may question whether paid advertisements help voters to make substantive assessments of the candidates. While such a concern has merit (especially when one examines many of Hart's advertisements that talk vaguely about the future, "new ideas," "new leadership"), often the advertisements focus on specific issues of the campaign. Mondale, for example, in a television advertisement in the New York primary stated:

In 1981 Reagan had a new idea about taxes. Huge tax breaks for the wealthy, virtually nothing for middle-income people. In the Chicago debate last week, my opponent had a similar new idea. He supported an additional tax increase of up to $600 a year on the middle class. I don't think it's right and I know it is not fair. It's time we stopped using the middle-income Americans to balance the national budget.

Another advertisement from the Dukakis campaign prior to Super Tuesday said the following:

Congressman Dick Gephardt has flip-flopped on a lot of issues. He has been both for and against Reaganomics, for and against raising the minimum wage, for and against freezing social security benefits. Congressman Dick Gephardt acts tough toward big corporations but takes their PAC money.

Mike Dukakis refuses PAC money, opposes Reaganomics, and supports a strong minimum wage and social security. You know where Mike Dukakis stands. Congressman Gephardt? He is still up in the air.

These types of advertisements are not uncommon and do focus on substantive concerns. In sum, this source of information should not be overlooked when assessing the type of information voters in primaries receive about the candidates.

Actually, there is some reason to believe that political advertisements in presidential primaries may influence voters' choices. A CBS-*New York Times* poll of likely voters on Super Tuesday lends some modest support to this contention. Among respondents who claimed to see Gephardt's commercials, 41 percent had a favorable opinion of him. In contrast, only 18 percent of likely voters who had not seen an advertisement by Gephardt viewed him favorably. A similar pattern emerged for attitudes toward Gore. I am not arguing that there is a clear cause-and-effect relationship, but the evidence is still suggestive.[8]

The arguments presented should ease the concerns of some critics that the news media's coverage of the "game aspect" prevents voters from making substantive judgments. While certainly the news media focus on these matters, it may be an inevitable part of *any* nominating system. Even in the old "mixed" system, the news media focused primarily on the winners and losers (see Table 6.1). From 1952 to 1968, over 80 percent of the headlines in the *New York Times* dealt with the game aspect. One headline in the *New York Times* following the 1952 New Hampshire primary demonstrates this continuity in coverage:

EISENHOWER DEFEATS TAFT,
KEFAUVER WINS OVER TRUMAN
IN NEW HAMPSHIRE'S PRIMARY

Of course, in the mixed system voters in primaries were much less influential in choosing candidates. But the point is that while one may prefer the news media to address other concerns, it is unlikely their coverage of the "game" aspect of the nominating process will change significantly.[9] Moreover, one could argue that any changes toward more "substantive" reporting could lessen the interest of voters in the campaign, resulting in an even less informed electorate than exists now—exactly the opposite outcome critics desire.

THE NEWS MEDIA AND VOTERS' PREFERENCES

A more serious concern about the news media is that their treatment of candidates directly influences who voters support in primaries. The findings in Chapter 5 certainly lend support to this claim. By providing favorable, unfavorable, or minimal coverage, the news media can alter the electorate's assessments of candidates. There is little doubt that the news media influence the choices of some voters. William Adams (1987) makes this point nicely by showing that the "winner" of the New Hampshire primary gains about 11 percent, on average, in nationwide support. This boost in support is presumably due to the favorable coverage the winner of that primary receives from the news media. Bartels (1985, 1987, 1988) has carefully documented that momentum exists in primaries, which suggests that the preferences of some voters react, at least in part, to how the news media cover candidates.

It makes sense that the news media's treatment of the contenders would influence the choices of many voters in primaries. The conditions in some contests are nearly ideal. First, there are often large numbers of candidates competing for the nomination, which forces journalists to give little or no coverage to dark horses.[10] The decisions about who to cover and who not to cover have a large effect on the prospects of the candidates. One reason the candidacies, for example, of Fred Harris, Reubin Askew, or Pete DuPont never got off the ground was because voters gained little information about them and hence did not give them careful consideration.

The second condition that increases the power of the news media is that many of the presidential hopefuls are not well-known figures among the electorate. These unknown contenders, Arterton (1984) observes, may "confuse voters, sending them to the mass media for information about [them]" (p. 3). This information is particularly important because it helps generate voters' first impressions of the candidates. So in 1984, voters' initial view of Gary Hart may have been of a relatively young candidate who had "new ideas" and offered "new leadership."

The third aspect of the nominating system that magnifies the news media's power is that many voters have weakly held preferences for candidates. Since the contests are intraparty affairs, partisan attachments cannot serve as an anchor to secure voters' choices. Voters may thus be likely to drift between candidates. To compound matters, candidates in primaries often do not differ greatly on issues, making it even harder for voters to form a strong preference. Bush and Dole, for instance, offered nearly "reflected images" of each other (Hoffman 1988). Tables 5.1 and 5.2 provide more systematic support for this contention. With an electorate that has weakly held preferences, favorable treatment by the news media may prove decisive in the choices of many voters. And in early contests where primaries are generally competitive, this effect assumes even greater importance.

The final aspect of the system that amplifies the news media's power is that New Hampshire leads off the primary season. By having only a single contest at the outset, the news media can focus heavily on the "winners," flooding them with coverage. For instance, after Hart's win in New Hampshire he was on the covers of *Time, Newsweek, People, New York,* and *The Economist,* not to mention the coverage he received from network television. Robinson (1978) estimates that the day following the 1976 New Hampshire primary the three networks dedicated 2,100 seconds of air time to the contest—nearly four times more coverage than was given to the New York primary held six weeks later. With this kind of coverage it is critical for a candidate to do well in New Hampshire. Otherwise, the contender receives little press, as Bruce Babbitt, Howard Baker, and John Glenn can attest. Robinson and Sheehan (1983) aptly call this process "journalistic triage." Candidates placed in the "hopeless" category will face an uphill battle to remain competitive in future primaries. On the other hand, contenders thought of as "likely" will continue to get attention that will help fuel efforts in upcoming primaries.

All these conditions generally exist when there is no incumbent seeking the nomination, which was the case with six of ten contests since 1972.[11] When, however, an incumbent president runs for reelection, the news media's power is greatly reduced as was the case in the Ford-Reagan or Carter-Kennedy contests. In these instances most voters in primaries had prior knowledge of the president. And given the electoral weight of the presidency, nearly all challengers will be serious, well-known challengers like Reagan and Kennedy. The news media, under such conditions, cannot as easily shape preferences as in the cases where unknown candidates are competing, since voters will already have information about their choices. Moreover, with fewer candidates running, the news media's decisions on whom to cover do not come into play.

While the news media have great influence in many races as outlined by these conditions listed above, it would still be hard to argue that the news media "select" nominees. For instance, the news media were writing Bush's political obituary following the 1988 Iowa caucuses. Yet despite this unfavorable coverage, he managed a resurrection by winning the New Hampshire primary in convincing fashion. This victory solidified his lead in the "Super Tuesday" states, which allowed him to oust Dole from the race for the nomination by the end of March. In 1980, Bush was on the other side of the fence. Arterton (1984) contends that:

George Bush benefited enormously in news coverage by his success in the Iowa caucuses. Polls at the time showed a marked shift toward Bush away from Reagan. Reagan strategists responded by actively and aggressively campaigning in New Hampshire, something they had intentionally minimized in Iowa. Although it is impossible to dissect how Reagan regained his support and won the New Hampshire primary, it is certainly clear that abundant and favorable horserace reporting was not sufficient to produce victory for Bush. (p. 200)

Journalists are just one actor in a complicated process. While the behavior of the news media was important to the rise of Hart and Carter, other conditions had to be present. This point is obvious, but all too often the critics paint the news media as an almost omnipotent force in the nominating process. To avoid overstating the power of the news media I shall provide some reasons why we should temper the claim that the news media, by shaping voters' preferences, "select" our presidential nominees.

First, the news media's coverage of the candidates is not arrived at independently. That is, the news media's assessments are a product of a number of factors—poll ratings, money raised, endorsements, views of party leaders, the contenders' own statements, votes cast in prior primaries or caucuses, and others. It is difficult to sort out how these factors affect journalists' coverage of candidates, but the findings in Table 3.2 suggest that the news media's coverage responds to such matters as competitiveness and spending by the candidates. Table 6.2 provides some additional evidence by showing that the news media's coverage of candidates in the year prior to the nomination corresponds to the contenders' poll ratings at the time. Specifically, there is a .69 correlation between the number of stories and the Gallup Poll standing of candidates in the year prior to the election since 1972. The strength of this relationship suggests that the news media pay some attention to objective measures of a candidate's standing such as public opinion polls.

Party leaders also influence the news media's assessment of the candidates. If party leaders view one candidate as the likely nominee, the news media's coverage will reflect that judgment. In 1984, Mondale was seen as the front-runner by the news media in part because much of the Democratic leadership supported his candidacy. Party leaders can also affect the criteria the news media use when deciding whether a candidate "won" or "lost" a primary. If, for instance, party leaders believe that a contender must "win" an upcoming primary, the news media will pick up on that decision and weave it into their coverage. In 1988, for instance, most analysts felt that Dukakis had to win the New Hampshire primary; failure to do so would have spelled disaster for him. This expectation was the product of the views of the news media, party leaders, and even the Dukakis camp. The point is that the news media do not operate in a vacuum; they respond to the political environment around them.[12]

Another reason to be cautious in our criticisms about the news media's role is that their influence is not new to the nomination of presidential candidates. In the previous nominating system the news media also made strategic assessments about prospective candidates, which in turn affected contenders' chances of gaining the nomination. David et al. (1960) argued that "[I]n deciding on their own allocation of news time and space, the mass media reflect their own judgments of the relative importance and newsworthiness of the respective candidates. Candidates that the media refuse to take seriously as news are likely to find their difficulties redoubled, while those who are given top news treatment take on the appearance of leaders" (p. 302). Stanley Kelley (1962) concurred: "In contests for nomination the treatment the media give candidates may have even more important consequences than it does in general election campaigns. It may serve as an indication to the public of the candidacies that are to be taken seriously and those that are not" (p. 311).

Data from Table 6.2 lend support to these observations. In contested races for the nomination from 1952 to 1968 there is about a .64 correlation between the Gallup ratings of candidates and the amount of coverage they received in the press in the year prior to the election. The strength of this relationship is about the same for the period between 1972 and 1988, suggesting that the connection between news media and poll ratings has remained much the same.

Further evidence that the news media are not new to the process can be found in Table 6.1. These data show that the *amount* of media attention given to the nominating process has not changed significantly since 1952. In competitive struggles for the nomination from 1952 to 1968, there were, on average, 58 front-page stories in the *New York Times* about the campaign from January 1st to the last primary in June (see Table 6.1), with the highest figure during that period coming in the 1952 Republican contest. From 1972 to 1988 the number of stories averaged 59. This figure does not even control for the increase in the number of primaries since the early 1970s. In short, journalists are not new actors in the selection process. Perhaps when there is a large number of possible nominees, the news media's coverage helps voters choose, regardless of the actual nominating arrangements.

Table 6.2
The News Media's Coverage of the Candidates in the Year Before the Election

	Number of Stories	Gallup Poll Rating
1952 Republicans		
Eisenhower	37	30
Taft	29	22
Stassen	7	10
Warren	1	13
1960 Democrats		
Kennedy	18	26
Johnson	16	12
Symington	6	4
Humphrey	8	6
Stevenson	4	29
1964 Republicans		
Rockefeller	27	28
Goldwater	44	38
Romney	8	16
1968 Republicans		
Nixon	14	39
Romney	32	25
Rockefeller	11	10
Reagan	7	11
1972 Democrats		
McGovern	12	5
Humphrey	6	21
Muskie	23	40
Jackson	16	6
1976 Democrats		
Humphrey	5	9
Wallace	9	15
Jackson	9	6
1980 Republicans		
Baker	8	10
Reagan	20	28
Dole	1	3
Bush	11	2
Connally	23	8
1984 Democrats		
Mondale	43	41
Hart	3	3
Glenn	30	24
Jackson	21	8
Hollings	3	1
Cranston	12	8
Askew	2	3

Table 6.2 Continued

1988 Republicans		
Bush	22	39
Dole	17	21
duPont	0	2
Haig	2	6
Kemp	16	8
Robertson	13	6
1988 Democrats*		
Babbitt	4	2
Biden	6	7
Dukakis	21	18
Gephardt	8	7
Gore	12	5
Jackson	42	18

*The Democratic field was a bit muddled. First, Hart dropped out in the middle of 1987 and then dropped back in at the end of the year. There were 26 stories about Hart and another 20 that concerned the Donna Rice incident. Second, there were a number of prominent Democrats who many thought might run: Cuomo (24 stories), Bradley (11 stories), and Nunn (11 stories).

The "number of stories" was arrived at by adding up the number of stories concerning the candidates in the Reader's Guide to Periodical Literature for the year prior to the election. The Gallup Poll data were from surveys conducted in June of that year, except for 1976 where the data were from a survey in August.

Source: Gallup Poll and compiled by author.

Some scholars suggest that the news media's influence was growing even before the reforms of the 1970s. David et al. (1960) observed that:

The election process for the Presidency has been a mass media phenomenon in the United States for generations, but, until recent decades, in the nominating process the most vital flows of information were largely handled through other means. With the coming of the presidential primaries and more open patterns of campaigning, the news of the nominating process became much more accessible to the mass media and they assumed a corresponding importance. (p. 301)

Timothy Crouse (1973) contends that the news media's coverage of campaigns was heavily influenced by Theodore White's *The Making of the President* series. The news media's increased importance, therefore, cannot solely be attributed to the recent proliferation of presidential primaries, which placed voters at center stage. Their influence in the nominations of candidates did not begin with the emergence of the current system, nor is it likely to end if the parties decrease the number and importance of primaries.

These points are important because all too often the news media's influence is judged in *absolute* terms. That is, the media are supposed to have "too much" influence. But it is difficult to know what constitutes "too much" influence. To avoid this problem one can employ a *relative* standard, that is, by determining whether the news media were important in previous nominating arrangements and drawing comparisons. While obviously we lack precise estimates, it appears likely that the news media will be influential in any nominating system. Journalists clearly play a bigger role in the process than they did 20 years ago. But the amount of the gain is unclear and we cannot be certain that the increase in the number of primaries has triggered this surge in power.

Finally, when assessing the news media's influence, it is possible that the decisions they make concerning how to cover candidates are not necessarily bad ones. Journalists appear to be relatively objective in their strategic assessments (Robinson and Sheehan 1983; Brady 1984). While party leaders might be better strategic actors, journalists rely on poll results, election returns, the views of party leaders, and the campaign strategy of the candidates when making assessments. The main fault of these reporters is that they are in a "rush" to make assessments (Arterton 1978). Often on the basis of one or two early contests a candidate will either sink or swim. Such early decisions are often unfair because with additional caucuses and primaries a candidate might be able to perform much better. But even when the news media exhibit great influence, some do not see that influence as completely bad. Matthews (1978), for example, is unsure that party leaders were better at winnowing out candidates: "Today . . . 'screening' is informally and imperfectly performed mostly by political reporters. In the past, this function was performed by established political party leaders and large campaign contributors. It is not self-evident to me that these groups were any wiser or more dedicated to the commonweal than the press" (p. 69).

CONCLUSION

While the news media's effect on voters in primaries has been the subject of much criticism, this discussion suggests that perhaps these complaints have been overstated. To begin with, the fact that the news media focus on the game aspect need not be a major cause for concern: voters appear to be making judgments on the basis of substantive matters anyway. They may be able to do so, in part, because the distinction between "game" and "substance" is unclear and, in part, because of the content of paid advertisements, which often goes unmentioned in discussions of the media's influence in primary elections. More important, arguments that the news media "select" nominees in the current system are overstated. First, journalists rely on the assessments of party leaders and other actors in the process when crafting their views. The news media can thus be thought of as a megaphone for the ideas and perceptions of others involved in the process. Second, one should keep in mind that the news media were important to the previous nominating arrangement, suggesting that journalists have been and are likely to remain important actors in the selection process.

Of course, one could argue that many of my arguments are simply looking "at the glass half full, rather than half empty." While such a claim may have merit, it is important to consider carefully the accuracy of the criticisms against the news media; otherwise one may be misled about the qualifications of voters in primaries to select candidates.

Nevertheless, these arguments do not mean that the news media's role is beneficial. When a large number of candidates compete, especially when some of the candidates are not well known to the public, the news media are important actors in the system and probably shape the preferences of many voters. Whether such influence means the news media are "too" important remains unclear. But it may be worth considering when and where the news media have influence and try to suggest changes in the system that reflect this information, as I shall attempt in the concluding chapter.

NOTES

1. A great deal of work focuses on this matter. See, for instance, Patterson (1980), Robinson and Sheehan (1983), Ranney (1983), Arterton (1984), Richard Joslyn (1984), Brady and Johnston (1987), Orren and Polsby (1987), and Bartels (1988).

2. Polsby (1980) offers a similar interpretation as represented by the title of his article, "The News Media as an Alternative to Party in the Presidential Selection Process."

3. This quote comes from a videotape of NBC Nightly News the day after the New Hampshire primary.

4. These data are from Brady and Johnston (1987), pp. 144–147. I added together the number of stories before and after the Iowa caucuses and calculated the relevant percentages.

5. Of course, partisanship provides cues in the general election, which makes the decision of whom to vote for different. But the point is that "horse race" journalism does not keep voters from making substantive evaluations of the candidates.

6. Orren and Polsby (1987) make a similar observation about the possible influence candidates' advertising might have on voters' preferences.

7. While these advertisements are not a random sample of all spots, there is

no reason to think that they misrepresent the general character of commercials in primaries. I thank Stanley Kelley and Mike Danielson for assistance in collecting advertisements from 1984.

8. These data appeared in a front page story in the *New York Times*, March 4th, 1988.

9. In recent years there has been some effort by news media to give more details about the candidates. For instance, the *New York Times* often runs a series of articles describing the candidates' strategies, views on issues, and personal background. While such coverage is not frequent, it may help provide some additional insights about the candidates. Robinson and Sheehan (1983) argue that the media appear to have made efforts to cover the issues better, especially in the television news.

10. The news media cannot give equal coverage to all candidates because they have only so many minutes (or column-inches) to present the candidates. Therefore, they pay less attention to those contenders they view as long shots. Arterton (1984) and Crouse (1973) provide much insight into the constraints under which the news media operate that force them to cover only the major contenders.

11. The cases are: 1972, 1976, 1984, and 1988 for the Democrats, and 1980 and 1988 for the Republicans.

12. Arterton (1984) provides a thoughtful account of the news media's relationship with other political actors.

═══ 7 ═══

A Few Rules of the Game

At this point we have a good deal of information about voters in primaries. How well these participants select candidates cannot be judged solely on the basis of the information presented so far, however. The rules governing the conduct of presidential primaries may affect the ability of voters in primaries to make good choices. For instance, a common complaint leveled against voters in primaries is that they cannot select "electable" candidates (see, for instance, Polsby 1983; Ranney 1975). The reasons offered in support of this claim are that voters are uninformed about the electability of potential nominees and that voters are unrepresentative of the rank and file. While Chapter 2 casts serious doubt on the accuracy of the latter, the former may have some merit, given the results in Chapter 4. I shall argue, however, that it is not necessarily the weaknesses of voters that prevent candidates with broad support from securing the nomination; it is rather the rules that may be preventing such contenders from capturing a majority of delegates.

This chapter recognizes that different rules can lead to different kinds of behavior by voters. Up to this point I have ignored, for the most part, how the rules may shape the way voters in primaries behave. This chapter and the next one will attempt to rectify that situation.

CAN VOTERS IN PRIMARIES CHOOSE CANDIDATES WITH BROAD SUPPORT?

As noted above, many scholars claim that the replacement of a politician-dominated system of presidential nominations by one dominated by rank-and-file voters has weakened the capacity of the national parties to nominate candidates with broad support.[1] On the surface at least there seems to be some merit to this criticism. Of the last eight competitive nominations, two of the standard bearers, Mondale and McGovern, went down to massive defeat in the general election. One of the reasons cited for these defeats is that these candidates were unable to appeal to enough voters to build broad coalitions. This problem of coalition building goes beyond just winning the general election because even if such a candidate manages to win the general election, this weakness becomes a handicap once the candidate is in office. Polsby (1983) contends that one of Carter's problems was that he was a factional candidate and not one who could build a broad enough consensus to govern the nation effectively. Of course, the lopsided defeats of Mondale and McGovern and Carter's difficulties can be attributed to many factors. But if relying on voters to choose nominees makes these problems more common, then there is cause for concern.

But what might cause this problem? Obviously, one could develop a number of possible hypotheses, such as the idea that voters simply lack the information to choose candidates with widespread support. While I cannot eliminate this potential explanation, it seems that primaries should actually be *particularly well suited* to picking candidates with broad support. The reason that primaries may be able to select such candidates is that these contests provide an opportunity to measure voters' preferences for candidates. In the "mixed" system, party leaders generally sought to pick the most electable candidate available. They accomplished this task by estimating which candidates voters would be most likely to support in November. These judgments, however, were far from flawless. One need only to recall the ill-fated candidacies of John Davis, Alfred Landon, and James Cox for examples of nominees who lacked broad support in the electorate. Presidential primaries, in contrast, can actually test candidates' popularity, and hence their potential electability. As Polsby (1960) once observed, presidential primaries can serve "as a means by which politicians inform themselves about the relative popularity of presidential aspirants" (p. 617). Thus, in principle, primaries may provide *more* reliable estimates of a candidate's ability to win votes than can party leaders.

The problem, however, is that the current system of primaries does not automatically produce nominees who are capable of doing well in the November election. Factional candidates may skillfully parlay narrow but intense support into a party nomination; or party regulars, who lack appeal to independents, may sweep to victory. This problem is especially worrisome when a large number of candidates compete for the nomination. In 1976, for instance, Jimmy Carter won less than 30 percent of the vote in both Iowa and New Hampshire. Yet because of the crowded field of candidates, he won both contests. It is hard to argue, however, that voters in these states were casting overwhelming support for the former governor. But because of the rules, Carter was able to parlay these narrow victories into national exposure, fueling his bid for the Democratic nomination.

Primaries, therefore, need to be designed in such a way to maximize the chances that a candidate who receives the most delegates (and hence, presumably, the nomination) will be someone with widespread appeal in the electorate. In this chapter I shall consider three rules that affect the assessment of the preferences of voters: the allocation of delegates, the ballot used by voters in primaries, and regulations specifying who can and cannot participate in primaries. As I examine each of these rules I shall suggest changes in them that should encourage a more accurate reading of candidates' popularity. Keep in mind that these rules only concern the ability of primaries per se to measure voters' preferences accurately. Other rules, like New Hampshire's role as the first primary, will be set aside until the concluding chapter.

VOTES AND DELEGATES

Since voters in primaries actually select delegates who, in turn, officially choose nominees, it is important to know how the vote in primaries translates into delegates. Different systems of allocation affect the number of delegates a candidate receives and hence affect how the preferences of voters are registered. If the allocation of delegates is to reflect accurately the popularity of candidates, the system must not skew the results in favor of a particular candidate by magnifying the size of the victory or loss.

There have been four basic methods of allocating delegates in primaries: proportional representation, winner-take-more, winner-take-all, and "loophole." A state using proportional representation allocates delegates among candidates in proportion to their share of the vote. The winner-take-more system, adopted for the Democratic contests in 1984 and 1988, allocates delegates to candidates by congressional district in proportion to their share of the vote, but the winner of the district receives a bonus delegate. The winner-take-all system gives all the state's delegates to the candidate who receives the most votes statewide. A "loophole" primary makes it possible for the winner to take all the delegates. The actual "loophole" will, however, vary a bit from state to state and also between election years.[2]

One way to examine how alternative methods of allocation might affect how votes are recorded is to see if different schemes would have changed the proportion of delegates a candidate received in past contests (Lengle and Shafer 1976; Hammond 1980; Pomper 1979; David and

Ceasar 1980). James Lengle and Byron Shafer (1976) argue, for instance, that in the 1972 race for the presidential nomination

the beneficiary of the power hidden in the rules of the game was Senator George McGovern. Most primaries offered by (congressional) District and Districted primaries maximized McGovern's strength. One simple shift, however, to generalized Winner-Take-All laws would have *minimized* that strength, in the process guiding a healthy plurality of delegates (along with the nomination?) to Senator Hubert Humphrey. A second change, to proportional representation, would have undercut both McGovern and Humphrey, leaving only Governor George Wallace to derive electoral satisfaction from primary rules. (p. 25)[3]

This argument assumes that under different rules the actions of McGovern (and other candidates) would have been the same. Behavior of candidates, however, "cannot be expected to be constant under different institutional arrangements" (David and Ceasar 1980, p. 36). If, for example, all states were winner-take-all, candidates might target resources in those states in which they had a chance. In a system of proportional representation, candidates might enter more contests since even a small proportion of the vote could yield a few delegates. In what follows I shall not speculate about how the different rules might have changed outcomes; instead I shall show how the candidates fared under each system and to what degree different rules affect the allocation of delegates and hence how the various systems recorded the preferences of voters.

Edward Tufte (1973) has provided a useful way to examine how different rules affect the translation of votes into delegates. In studying the relationship between seats and votes in legislative contests, Tufte posited a simple linear model

$$Y = A + B1(X) + E$$

where Y is the percentage of seats for a particular party and X is the percentage of votes for that party. One can adapt this equation to the issue at hand by making Y the percentage of delegates for a candidate and X the percentage of votes for that candidate. This linear equation, so modified, yields three politically meaningful numbers that can be compared over time, between parties, between candidates, and between allocation systems.[4] The first is the regression slope or what Tufte calls "swing ratio" or "responsiveness." If the swing ratio is 2, that means for every 1 percent change in the vote there is a 2 percent change in the proportion of delegates awarded a given candidate. The second is the "bias," which measures the percentage of votes necessary to receive 50 percent of the delegates. These two numbers provide information on how well the various systems translate votes (i.e., preferences) into delegates and the extent to which certain candidates were helped or hurt by the rules. The third measure, which I shall term the "threshold" (the x-intercept of the regression line), shows the percentage of votes necessary to receive any delegates at all. The threshold figure is important to candidates such as Jesse Jackson and Pat Robertson who want, perhaps for bargaining purposes, to stay in the presidential race until the convention even though they have little chance of winning the nomination themselves.[5]

A system of allocation would record votes accurately if candidates were awarded delegates in strict proportion to their share of the primary vote; that is, the responsiveness would be 1 with a bias of 50 percent and a threshold of 0 percent. No system in actual use is likely to measure the preferences of voters so accurately. As Tufte (1973) argues, "arrangements for translating votes into legislative seats almost always work to benefit the party winning the largest share of the votes" (p. 540).[6] Nevertheless, this ideal outcome provides a benchmark by which to judge the different systems and how candidates profited from various ways of apportioning delegates.

Table 7.1 reports the responsiveness, bias, threshold, and linear fit (R-squared) of the allocation of delegates from 1972 to 1988. As one can see, the proportion of delegates candidates receive is not an accurate reflection of their votes. Some contenders had their share of the vote greatly magnified by the rules allocating delegates while other candidates suffered from the rules. In 1972, for instance, McGovern benefited from the rules of the Democratic Party, as Lengle and Shafer (1976) suggested. McGovern typically needed only about 31 percent of the vote to receive 50 percent of the delegates, while Senator Humphrey needed about 50 percent and Governor Wallace about 40 percent of the vote to secure half of the delegates.

The rules governing the 1984 Democratic nomination contest benefited Walter Mondale, as the former vice-president's strategists intended. He typically needed about 38 percent of the vote to receive 50 percent of the delegates. The swing ratio for Mondale was 1.39, a figure similar to that for Hart, but larger than that for Jackson (1.2). Jackson also generally needed more votes than either of his rivals to receive 50 percent of the delegates. During the 1984 prenomination campaign, Jesse Jackson complained that the system of delegate apportionment treated him unfairly.[7] His complaints are clearly warranted. Compared with Mondale, Jackson had a higher threshold, lower responsiveness, and a less-favorable bias.

The Republicans in 1988 had the least accurate system of allocating delegates. Bush needed only 15 percent of the vote to get 50 percent of the delegates. This low proportion of votes reflects the fact that Bush

Table 7.1
The Relationship Between Delegates and Votes

CASE	N@	RESPON-SIVENESS	BIAS	THRESHOLD	R-SQUARED
Democrats, 1972					
All cases	50	1.92	37.7%	11.7%	.68
McGovern	14	2.30	30.7%	9.0%	.73
Humphrey	14	1.33	50.8%	13.2%	.49
Wallace	13	1.81	40.3%	12.7%	.73
Loophole	30	1.80	38.1%	10.3%	.72
Democrats, 1976					
All cases	61	1.23	43.1%	2.5%	.85
Carter	21	1.05	40.1%	7.6%	.69
Udall	12	1.15	47.3%	3.9%	.92
PR local$	46	1.16	45.0%	1.9%	.95
PR state	22	1.14	46.1%	2.2%	.97
Loophole	15	1.50	38.5%	5.1%	.71
Republicans, 1976					
All Cases	38	2.01	49.7%	24.8%	.55
Ford	19	2.14	45.9%	22.7%	.63
Reagan	19	1.97	53.6%	28.2%	.57
Loophole	14	3.71	50.2%	36.6%	.64
PR$	20	1.28	49.6%	10.5%	.75
Republicans, 1980					
All cases	69	1.46	44.4%	10.1%	.87
Reagan	27	1.01	33.3%	-16.4%	.61
Bush	27	1.54	44.2%	11.8%	.77
Loophole	26	1.66	43.6%	13.6%	.82
PR	32	1.22	45.1%	4.1%	.93
Democrats, 1980					
All cases	61	1.23	45.6%	4.9%	.93
Carter	30	1.22	44.6%	3.7%	.92
Kennedy	30	1.16	46.6%	3.5%	.90
PR	59	1.19	45.6%	3.6%	.95
Democrats, 1984					
All cases	72	1.44	43.0%	8.2%	.77
Mondale	24	1.39	38.3%	2.4%	.50
Hart	24	1.38	45.5%	9.3%	.65
Jackson	24	1.20	50.7%	9.0%	.91
Loophole	21	1.93	42.0%	16.0%	.67
PR	39	1.30	43.3%	4.8%	.92
W-Take-More$	12	1.61	40.8%	9.8%	.76
Republicans, 1988*					
All cases	56	1.70	40.5%	11.2%	.81
Bush	19	.74	15.0%	-52.6%	.14
Dole	19	1.10	54.5%	10.0%	.30
Robertson	15	.17	291.0%	-3.3%	.02
PR	23	1.20	45.9%	4.3%	.95
W-Take-All$	25	2.20	39.1%	16.4%	.85
Loophole	8	1.50	41.3%	8.0%	.83

Table 7.1 Continued

Democrats, 1988					
All cases	91	1.40	41.6%	5.9%	.91
Dukakis	31	1.40	41.2%	5.5%	.94
Jackson	32	1.20	45.9%	4.3%	.79
Gore	18	1.40	41.4%	5.7%	.95
Gephardt	8	1.60	39.4%	8.1%	.95
PR	55	1.20	44.8%	3.1%	.94
W-Take-More	23	1.50	40.9%	7.5%	.91
Loophole	13	1.70	41.7%	12.3%	.88

@"N" represents the number of vote and delegate shares by
candidate.
$"PR Local" signifies those states that allocated delegates
proportionally to the candidates at the congressional district
level. "PR" stands for proportional representation. "W-Take-
More" stands for states that allocate delegates proportionally,
but provide a bonus delegate for the candidate who wins the most
votes in the congressional district. "W-Take-All" indicates
states that allow the winner of the primary to take all the
delegates. "Loophole" systems generally permit some form of
winner-take-all.

*The data from the Republican race in 1988 cover only the period
where Dole was actively campaigning. After his withdrawal, Bush
was winning nearly all the delegates in each primary. Under
those conditions the rules make little difference, providing
little insight into how well they measure the preferences of
voters.

Source: <u>Congressional Quarterly Weekly Report</u>.

was able to translate narrow wins at the polls into large victories in the share of delegates. While Dole suffered under this arrangement, Robertson fared even worse. On Super Tuesday, for instance, Robertson received nearly 14 percent of the votes yet won only 1 percent of the delegates. Dole gathered nearly a quarter of the vote on that day but secured less than 14 percent of the delegates. Bush, in contrast, used 56.5 percent of the vote to garner nearly 85 percent of the delegates. While Super Tuesday was a major victory for Bush by most standards, the rules magnified it even more.

Of the various methods of allocating delegates, it is no surprise that proportional representation best reflects a candidate's share of the vote. In each year the states using proportional representation had a responsiveness near 1 and a bias approaching 50 percent. Overall, the rules for the 1980 Democratic nomination contest produced the most accurate system so far: responsiveness was 1.23, bias 45.6 percent, and threshold 4.9 percent. The reason for these results is that almost all states employed a proportional-representation system that year. There was also little difference in swing ratio or bias between Carter and Kennedy: Carter's swing ratio was 1.22 while Kennedy's was 1.16; the bias suggests only a slight edge to Carter—44.6 percent to 46.6 percent.

In short, allocating delegates in proportion to a candidate's share of the vote is the best way for primaries to record the preferences of voters accurately.[8] The fraction of delegates awarded candidates under this arrangement roughly reflects their share of the vote. Other rules skew the results. Parties often write the rules, however, to favor particular kinds of candidates. It is difficult to separate the "feelings about changes in the rules from their [the rule makers] policy and candidate preferences" (Ranney 1975, p. 144). A major reason for the introduction of the "winner-take-more" rule in 1984, for example, was to diminish the chances of dark horses and enhance the odds favoring the front-runners, Mondale and Kennedy. But if the parties want to have an accurate reading of a candidate's popularity, then proportional representation seems to be the most desirable system.

THE BALLOT

Some would argue that primaries, regardless of the rules governing the allocation of delegates, cannot measure the preferences of voters very well. John Kellet and Kenneth Mott (1977) argue that "the primaries force a choice upon the voters. From an often large field of contenders, we are allowed to support only one. In cases where several candidates may espouse similar views and attract the same followers, the voters must divide their support among them, making it possible for a less popular person to win" (p. 529). Polsby (1983) expands on this assessment: "Second choice candidates enjoying widespread approval are unable to get into a game in which only first choices are counted. This becomes a problem because all first choice candidates of some voters are minimally acceptable to other voters—conceivably even to large numbers of voters to whom the party wants to appeal in the general election" (p. 165).

These criticisms are justified. In a large field of candidates, a contender can often win a primary with 30 to 40 percent of the vote. Yet 60 to 70 percent of voters may not support—or may even greatly dislike— the candidate who wins the primary.[9] This criticism, however, questions the desirability of allowing only first preferences to be expressed, *not* the direct primary. As Duncan Black (1957) argued, "the effect of the single vote is to suppress evidence of all preferences felt by the voter except his first preference for a single candidate" (p. 62). In this section, therefore, I shall argue that the preference ballot should replace the current ballot since it offers the best way for primaries to measure accurately the preferences of voters for candidates.[10]

The preference ballot, or the "alternative vote," allows each voter to rank candidates from first to last choice.[11] If no candidate wins a majority of first-place votes, then the candidate finishing last is dropped and his or her supporters go to their second preference. The elimination of candidates continues until a candidate receives a majority of votes. Under this system voters explicitly list their preferences, allowing parties to identify the second and third choices of the electorate. Consequently, candidates with only a small but intense following would not be able to win a primary. Only those candidates with broad support could, then, emerge victorious from a primary.

Some argue, however, that preference voting poses problems that make it an unattractive alternative. One potential weakness of preference voting is that the plurality winner could be eliminated after a series of vote transfers, upsetting that candidate's supporters and making party unity difficult. Second, the candidate who is most acceptable may not be chosen if that candidate finished a close last and hence was eliminated (Brams and Fishburn 1983).

The first criticism is a hybrid of correct and incorrect claims. It is true that preference voting could eliminate potential plurality winners, but only if the plurality winners had little or no support outside their narrow circle of voters. Thus, McGovern, the plurality winner in 1972, might not have been nominated in 1972 because many of the 70 percent of voters who did not support him strongly disliked him. But the elimination of plurality winners with narrow bases of support need not hamper party unity; it could, potentially, make it easier by ensuring that whoever did win the nomination would have broad support within the party. If, however, one takes the case of Jesse Jackson, a different story might emerge. It is likely that under this proposed system Jackson would have won far fewer primaries than he did in 1988. If so, he would surely have cried foul, creating disunity within the party. A situation like Jackson's is worrisome. But one must remember that the main purpose of preference voting is to secure candidates who have some support among as many voters as possible. The system, therefore, seeks to prevent factions in the party from forcing their choice on unwilling majorities. Critics who object to this feature of the preference ballot are thus claiming, in effect, that the feelings of intense minorities are more important than those of majorities. Whatever may be said for that position on normative grounds, it is not one that is well calculated for coalition building and winning general elections.

In addition, the plurality winners need not represent the feelings of *intense* minorities. In many cases, a plurality winner may emerge only because of the particular field of candidates. For example, one liberal in a field of a half a dozen moderates is likely to emerge as a plurality winner even though any of several moderates might have much broader and perhaps more intense appeal in the party. That preference voting would prevent such plurality victories is its strength rather than its weakness.

The second criticism does identify a potential problem for the preference system. In a multicandidate race, the elimination of the candidate with the fewest first-place votes could result in the elimination of the candidate with the broadest support. Steven Brams and Peter Fishburn cite the Senate race in New York in 1970 as an example. In that race, James Buckley, Richard Ottinger, and Charles Goodell sought the Senate seat. Under a system of preference voting, Goodell would have been eliminated since he finished last in the race. Conceivably, however, he might have beaten either Buckley or Ottinger in a two-candidate contest. Such situations, however, are not common in primaries. In multicandidate primaries, distant finishers are generally candidates with little support. Rarely does one see three candidates tightly bunched as in the case of that 1970 Senate election in New York. In 1984, for instance, Jesse Jackson finished last in most of the contests. He was a factional candidate with considerably less support than Hart and Mondale. In many struggles for the nomination the number of candidates has been quite large, such as in 1972, 1976, 1984, and 1988 for the Democrats, and in 1980 and 1988 for the Republicans. But many of these candidates who finished out of the running have had only a small following and thus were not competitive with the front runners. Such names as Fred Harris, Reubin Askew, Birch Bayh, Paul Simon, and Pat Robertson spring to mind. Nonetheless, this problem may arise from time to time, which means that there is some potential for error in the way the preference ballot measures preferences.

This chance of error, however, is far outweighed by the possible benefits of this ballot. A major advantage of preference voting is that strategic voting is discouraged (Lakeman 1970, pp. 71–73). When voters register only their first preference, there is incentive for voters to consider the chances of candidates to win as well as their actual preferences. When explicitly ranking preferences, however, voters need not worry about wasting a vote since their second choice counts if their first choice is eliminated. Thus voters will have the incentive to support their most preferred candidate, increasing the ability of primaries to measure their preferences accurately.

An additional benefit of this system is that the news media would no longer be responsible for estimating the depth of support a candidate has in the electorate. Polsby (1980), for instance, complains that under the "new participatory rules" the "second choices are the property of the media elites to distribute," which gives them additional power to "interpret" the results (p. 62). Under the preference ballot, voters would be supplying that information in the voting booth. Thus the preference ballot may reduce the power of the news media to determine "winners" and "losers."

Another advantage of preference voting is that it asks voters to think in terms they are well accustomed to. Voters can easily rank preferences and often do so. When confronted with a series of options, people often rank them: "I'd rather visit Josie and Fred than go shopping, but I do not want to watch television." Data confirm this argument. Many of the 1984 exit polls canvassed the second preferences of voters in primaries. Over 75 percent of voters generally had a second preference, suggesting that they could act in the manner I advocate. In short, since voters probably have a number of preferences, we should ask them and by so doing obtain better information about them.

At this point I have advocated two reforms for presidential primaries: allocate delegates to candidates in proportion to their shares of the vote, and adopt a preference ballot. Under these two changes, if one candidate receives 50 percent or more first-place votes, the delegates would be allocated proportionally to all contenders. But if no candidate won at least 50 percent of the vote, a likely possibility in early primaries, then the last-place finisher would be eliminated and that candidate's supporters would be given to their second preference. This process would continue until one candidate has 50 percent of the vote. At that point delegates would be allocated proportionally to the remaining candidates.[12] These reforms would prevent candidates with narrow bases of support from winning primaries, because a candidate must have at least some degree of support from 50 percent of the electorate to win a primary. And at the same time, the proportional representation rule assures that all "serious" candidates win a share of the delegates commensurate with their share of the vote. Consequently, the combination of these two rules should allow for an accurate assessment of the breadth of a candidate's support.

Since some of the exit polls from the 1984 presidential primaries asked voters their second choices, one can see how this reform might affect the measurement of voters' preferences. When using voters' second choices, the plurality winner remains victorious under the "preference" system. The margin of victory was, however, altered. For the most part, Mondale fared much better under this arrangement since he was generally the second choice of most of Jesse Jackson's supporters. Perhaps if this rule had been in place the bitter struggle between Hart and Mondale would have been lessened with stronger showings by the former vice-president. One, of course, can only speculate on the possible implications. But in any case this kind of system would have provided additional information about Mondale's, Hart's, and Jackson's support—an attractive feature if one seeks to nominate candidates with broad support.

WHO SHOULD VOTE IN PRESIDENTIAL PRIMARIES?

While accurately determining the breadth of support for a candidate is important for selecting electable nominees, we must also decide who should be allowed to vote in primaries. That is, should participation be limited to only partisans? Or should independents and members of the opposing party be allowed to participate? By permitting only certain segments of the electorate to participate, one may influence the kinds of candidates chosen. Thus, when trying to select nominees with broad support, we need to decide whose preferences should be measured.

The states have differed in their answers to this question. In general, there have been four basic types of rules governing eligibility to vote in primaries. One allows any registered voter to participate in a primary—the "open" primary. A second allows any registered voter to participate, providing that individual declares his or her partisanship at the polling booth. In a third kind of primary, registered independents may vote in either party's primary, but voters registered with one of the parties are limited to their own party's contest (I refer to this type of system as "semiclosed"). The last type is one in which only voters registered as members of a party can participate in that party's primary—the so-called "closed" primary.[13]

A central issue facing these rules concerns the possible effects of "crossover" voting.[14] The McGovern-Frasier Commission (1970) argued, for instance, that "a full opportunity for all Democrats to participate is diluted if members of other parties are allowed to participate in the selection of Delegates to the Democratic National Convention" (p. 47). The general view is that crossover voting is counterproductive to the interests of the party since independents and members of the opposing party are given a say in a strictly partisan matter.

Using the CBS/*New York Times* and ABC/*Washington Post* exit polls, I investigate whether independents and members of the opposition's party have different preferences from those of partisans, how frequently "crossover" voting occurs, and whether such participation "dilutes" the selection process.

Table 7.2 presents preferences of voters for candidates, controlling for partisanship. Independents often prefer different candidates from partisans. In 1976, Ronald Reagan received the support of a higher proportion of independent voters than of Republican voters. Of the nine cases for which I have data, only in New Hampshire and California did Reagan do worse among independents than among Republicans. At times the differences were substantial. In Indiana, the independents and Democrats gave Reagan his margin of victory: among Republicans, Reagan lost 54.5 percent to 45.5 percent to Ford, but independents gave Reagan a 57.3 percent to 42.7 percent edge over Ford, and Democrats supported

Table 7.2
The Preferences of Voters in Presidential Primaries Controlling for Partisanship

	REPUBLICANS	INDEPENDENTS	DEMOCRATS
Democrats, 1976			
Carter (n=10)	40.2%	36.6%	38.5%
Udall (n=6)	19.4%	29.2%	27.2%
Jackson (n=5)	23.8%	16.3%	19.0%
Wallace (n=7)	19.6%	15.5%	16.5%
Republicans, 1976			
Ford (n=9)	58.0%	48.8%	49.1%
Reagan (n=9)	42.0%	51.2%	50.9%
Democrats, 1980			
Brown (n=5)	8.6%	11.1%	6.3%
Carter (n=9)	57.2%	44.4%	50.4%
Kennedy (n=9)	27.5%	42.0%	44.3%
Republicans, 1980			
Anderson(n=5)	16.0%	31.5%	41.3%
Reagan (n=8)	58.7%	43.9%	41.8%
Bush (n=8)	26.2%	30.3%	27.1%
Democrats, 1984			
Hart (n=17)	47.4%	45.8%	35.6%
Jackson(n=15)	6.8%	15.3%	20.3%
Mondale(n=17)	24.8%	24.3%	39.9%

Percentages are the average share of the vote each candidate received in the primaries for each category of self-identifiers.

Source: CBS/New York Times and ABC/Washington Post exit polls.

Reagan over Ford 74.6 percent to 25.4 percent. When he sought the Republican nomination in 1980, John Anderson was more popular among Democrats and independents than among members of his own party. Anderson actually won among independent voters in Republican primaries in Massachusetts, Wisconsin, and Illinois, though he did not win any of these contests.

In the 1976 and 1980 Democratic primaries, independents did not differ consistently from Democratic identifiers. In New Hampshire in 1976, Morris Udall finished first among Democratic identifiers, while among independents and Republicans Carter won. In Wisconsin and Michigan Udall won among independents, though he lost the primary. In the 1980 Kennedy-Carter race, there was no consistent beneficiary of independents' support. In 1980 Governor Brown did better among independents than Democrats, but this performance still could not make him a serious

Table 7.3
The Partisan Makeup of the Electorate in Presidential Primaries
Under Different Rules

	REPUBLICANS	INDEPENDENTS	DEMOCRATS
	Democratic Primaries		
Open (n= 3)	6.3%	28.6%	65.1%
Closed (n=14)	3.3%	21.1%	75.6%
Semi-closed (n= 8)	3.0%	30.5%	66.6%
Declare Polls# (n=11)	4.8%	23.7%	71.5%
	Republican Primaries		
Open (n= 4)	51.5%	36.6%	12.0%
Closed (n= 4)	73.8%	22.6%	3.6%
Semi-closed (n= 5)	66.7%	29.6%	3.7%
Declare Polls# (n= 4)	69.1%	26.3%	4.6%

These data are an average of the partisan breakdown in each
type of primary in 1976, 1980, and 1984.

#In these primaries voters must declare that they are partisans
of that party in order to vote.

Source:CBS/New York Times and ABC/Washington Post exit polls.

challenger. In 1984, however, Hart fared much better among independents than Mondale.

There is little doubt that independents and members of the opposing
party can alter the outcome of primary elections. But even in "closed"
primaries in which only "party members" are supposed to participate,
self-identified independents and partisans of the opposition party still
constitute a sizable segment of the electorate (see Table 7.3). Differing
requirements for voting do not appear to have a large effect on the composition of electorates in primaries.[15] Among "closed" Democratic primaries, 75.6 percent of the electorate labeled themselves Democrats. In
"semiclosed" contests, this proportion declines to 66.6 percent.[16] For
"open" contests, the proportion is 65.1 percent. The Republican figures
tell a similar story, though in the case of "open" primaries more non-
Republican voters participated. The figures are 73.8 percent, 66.7 percent, and 51.5 percent for "closed," "semi-closed," and "open" primaries, respectively. In the 1980 Wisconsin Republican primary, 57.5
percent of the electorate were either Democrats or independents—the

highest proportion of nonpartisans among all the states. This high proportion of non-Republicans was surely due, in part, to Anderson's appeal to independents and Democrats.

The question becomes which of these rules would be the most likely to yield candidates with broad support. Given this objective, an argument can be made for encouraging independents and partisans from the opposition's party to participate in primaries. When choosing a candidate in the now-defunct mixed system, party leaders typically sought a candidate who could win the support not only from their partisans but also from independents and weak partisans of the other party. Recall the statement by Key (1964) I referred to in the second chapter: "Each party leadership must maintain the loyalty of its own standpatters; it must also concern itself with the great block of voters uncommitted to either party as well as those who may be weaned away from the opposition" (p. 220). Eisenhower's nomination in 1952 can be largely attributed to the belief of many Republican delegates that he could attract independent and Democratic support that Taft could not. Since neither party constitutes a majority of the electorate, winning the general election requires a candidate to gain votes from citizens who do not identify with that party. Certainly the Republican success in recent presidential elections can be attributed to that party's ability to attract independents and defectors from the Democratic party.

So if parties want to nominate electable candidates and they use primaries to choose such nominees, there are good reasons for making certain that the candidates they select are attractive to independents and supporters of the opposition. It is unlikely that independents would "raid" a party's primary to vote for their least-favorite candidate to undermine that party's chances in the general election. A more likely reason for independents (or even partisans of the other party) to vote in a partisan primary is that they found a candidate they would be willing to support in November.[17] Certainly the support Anderson and Wallace received from outside their own parties is consistent with this argument. Moreover, the 1984 Democratic primaries provided an excellent opportunity for Republicans to "raid," since Ronald Reagan was running unopposed. Yet there was no increase in such raiding in 1984. In 1976 and 1980 the fraction of Republicans in the "declare-at-poll" Democratic primaries was 5 percent, while in 1984 it actually declined to 4.6 percent.

In short, political parties should not worry about trying to limit participation only to partisans. It is in the interest of parties to encourage independents and potential defectors from the other party to participate in its primary, since knowing the preferences of these "swing" voters is useful when trying to select a nominee who has broad support. Parties should thus adopt some form of the "open" or "declare-at-polls" primary to govern the participation in these contests.[18]

CONCLUSION

As written in the initial section of this chapter, the rules governing primaries, not the voters in them, may be responsible for candidates with narrow bases of support winning the nomination. The evidence and arguments presented above offer support for that contention. To increase the chances that voters in primaries select candidates with widespread support, these intraparty struggles should rely on proportional representation schemes to allocate delegates, adopt a preference ballot, and allow independents and partisan defectors to participate in primaries.

The party does, however, have other concerns besides picking candidates with the most support. For instance, parties seek to choose an acceptable candidate quickly so as to avoid dividing the party. The proportional representation rule, for example, might keep contenders in the race longer than under a system that favors the winner. In 1988, for instance, Dole might have been able to stay in the race longer if the GOP had relied more on allocating delegates proportionally. Such prolonged candidacies can undermine party unity.[19] Also, allowing independents and partisans of the opposing party to participate may be seen by loyal partisans as undercutting the values of the party. If disillusioned, the "core" party supporters might be less willing to work for the party and contribute money to its campaign treasury.[20] Finally, a preference ballot could confuse voters (especially the poorly educated ones) and lessen turnout in the short run, which could potentially lead to voters who are highly unrepresentative of the rank and file selecting nominees.[21] Thus, when considering changes in the rules governing presidential primaries, such concerns must be balanced.

The more important lesson in this chapter, however, is that the rules governing presidential primaries need to be considered when assessing the characteristics of voters. Perhaps if additional rules were changed, then other weaknesses in the current system might be minimized. In the concluding chapter I shall consequently propose changes in the rules that take account of both the strengths and weaknesses of voters when choosing candidates.

NOTES

1. The term *broad support* is quite vague. When, for instance, does a candidate possess broad support? The proportion of the vote a candidate receives in the general election is a problematic measure since that percentage is related to a number of things such as economic conditions, events in the international arena, the effectiveness of his or her campaign, and the popularity of the opponents. One might instead use the favorability ratings of the candidates. Under

this approach, nominees with broad support should have high favorability ratings among the electorate even if they lose the general election. While this measure has some appeal, when does one measure the attitudes of voters? In January 1984, for instance, Mondale was viewed favorably by 42 percent of the public and unfavorably by 28 percent. By November the proportion had changed to 39 percent favorable and 48 percent unfavorable. In 1980, Carter experienced similar shifts in his favorability ratings. The point here is that a candidate who looks popular during the nomination may prove to be unpopular by the time of the general election. It is difficult to predict exactly how the public will view a candidate on the first Tuesday in November. As one can see, this concept is sticky.

In this chapter I am setting aside this matter and instead accepting the notion that recent candidates have often lacked broad support in the electorate.

2. This classification does not take account of all the variations in the rules for primaries since individual states often introduce slight differences. For example, the minimum share of the vote necessary to qualify for delegates often varies between states. Paul David and James Ceasar (1980) note that "despite the increased standardization in selection procedure that has taken place over the past decade (especially in the Democratic party), each state nomination race remains in many respects unique, colored by its own laws, party rules, traditions and political culture." Nonetheless, my four categories encompass the major differences.

3. Jack Hammond (1980) disagrees with Lengle and Shafer's conclusion, arguing that they biased their results by excluding California and New Mexico from the analysis.

4. While the linear equation provides useful indicators of how well preferences are being recorded, a potential problem arises when the relationship between the share of delegates and the share of the vote is not strictly linear. A small proportion of the vote may yield no delegates while a large proportion of the vote may bring an even bigger proportion of delegates than the vote share indicates. Systems other than proportional representation provide the winners of the primaries more delegates than their proportion of the vote indicates. If the relationship is not linear then the regression results may yield biased estimates. If one plots the proportion of delegates by the proportion of votes, however, the relationship for most years is quite linear.

5. Note that the bias and threshold are directly related to each other since they both are a product of the x-intercept. I report them separately because they are useful indicators in assessing the allocation rules.

6. Douglas Rae (1971) and Enid Lakeman (1970) concur with Tufte (1973) that the winner's share of legislative seats is often exaggerated because of electoral laws, especially under the "first-past-the-post" system.

7. See the *New York Times*, April 24th, May 11th, and May 24th, 1984, for articles reporting Jackson's complaints.

8. Rae (1971) and Lakeman (1970) reached similar conclusions when examining how election laws affect the votes-to-seat ratio.

9. Numerous studies document this problem; see Black (1957), Lakeman (1970), Polsby (1983), Dennis Mueller (1979), Brams and Fishburn (1983), and Joslyn (1976).

10. A commonly discussed alternative to first-preference voting is approval

voting. A number of scholars have supported this system; see Brams and Fishburn (1983), Kellet and Mott (1977), Gerald DeMaio and Douglas Muzzio (1981), and Joslyn (1976). Approval voting, however, does not allow voters to indicate their intensity of preferences, only the range of preferences. This ballot consequently provides less information about voters' preferences than preference voting. Moreover, strategic concerns may enter into voters' decisions. See Niemi (1984) and Niemi and Bartels (1984) for intelligent discussions of this weakness of approval voting.

11. See Lakeman (1970) for a useful account of the alternative vote, Chapter 3.

12. The 50 percent cutoff is not just an arbitrary stipulation. In electoral systems using the preference ballot it is the threshold used for identifying a winner (Lakeman 1970).

13. Although this four-way breakdown ignores some differences that exist between states, it nonetheless captures the basic options parties and states can use in determining who can participate in primaries.

14. Perhaps the earliest study of crossover voting was Overacker (1926). More recent studies are R. O. Hedlund (1977–78), David Adamany (1976), Hedlund et al. (1982), and Priscilla Southwell (1988).

15. The likely reason that these rules have only a limited effect on the partisan composition of the electorate is that they do not act as major barriers to participation. To vote, for instance, in a "closed" primary, all a voter has to do is register with the party. And this act does not provide reliable information about true partisanship (Ranney 1978, p. 221). Thus, while the "closed" primary provides more barriers to participation than these other three rules, it is still not enough of a barrier to prevent crossover voting.

16. There were two surveys in which the partisanship question was not used. Instead, a question concerning party registration was used. When these cases are eliminated the difference becomes 71.8 percent to 67.8 percent, not a major one.

17. Overacker (1926) came to a similar conclusion in her study of presidential primaries: "A careful study of the cases where the members of one party have participated in the primary of the other party . . . lends no color to the claim of the opponents of the "open" primary that voters go into the opposing party to throw their vote to the weakest candidates, or the candidates whom they think will be the most easily beaten in the election. In every case they have been motivated by a genuine interest in, and support of, the candidate for whom they voted" (p. 98).

18. One might argue that given the evidence in Table 7.3 changing the rules would have little influence on the partisan composition of primary electorates. While it is true that it may not always make a large difference, there is at least the potential for all registered voters to participate in a primary if they happen to be motivated by a particular candidate. Consequently, if a candidate has a great deal of support outside of the party, there would be an opportunity for it to be expressed.

19. One of the common concerns about primaries is that they create divisiveness within the party (see Kenney and Rice 1987b). Divisiveness should not, however, pose a problem for my "reformed" primaries. I suspect that the chances

of divisiveness may actually be somewhat reduced under my proposed arrangement. The reformed-primary system would allocate delegates in proportion to the candidate's share of the vote while using a preference ballot. This combination of rules may help reduce the possibility of hard-fought multicandidate primaries. First and perhaps most important, my rules would tend to prevent candidates who have narrower bases of support from winning primaries, because a candidate must have at least some support among 50 percent of the electorate. Without the resulting media coverage and extra delegates accorded a winner, such candidates may be less willing (and less able) to carry out a protracted battle for the nomination. Second, my proposed system would provide few if any delegates to the distant finishers because when no candidate receives 50 percent of the vote the preference ballot eliminates the candidate with the fewest votes. Thus, the rules may encourage candidates with little support to withdraw (and may even discourage these types of candidates from undertaking their long-shot campaigns) since they would be securing so few delegates. The remaining candidates may be locked in a competitive and possibly divisive struggle, but no more so than have been recent contenders for the nomination. Finally, since these rules attempt to reflect each candidate's popularity and are not designed to favor specific candidates, there may be fewer battles over the rules, as we saw in the 1984 Democratic nomination. (Though, of course, certain kinds of candidates will be helped under my system. But at least the rules were not written to favor a specific candidate, as has been the case in recent years.)

20. This possibility is unlikely, however. If candidates have broad support, they should be strong contenders in the general election. With a chance to win, party regulars may be more likely to help the party in the November election than when the candidate has only an outside shot at winning.

21. Actually, voters may not be confused by the preference ballot. As mentioned above, CBS/*New York Times* exit polls asked voters for their second preferences. Over 75 percent of voters have a second preference, suggesting that such a change need not confuse them. And if voters knew that additional preferences would be canvassed, many of them would make the necessary calculations, suggesting that those with no second choice might dwindle even further.

═8═

A Proposal for Reform

The findings in this study present a mixed picture about how well voters in primaries choose presidential candidates. Under some conditions these participants prove to be weak selectors, yet under other conditions they appear to be capable decision-makers. Some of the problems confronting the current system arise not because of the inability of voters in primaries to choose candidates well, but because of the rules in the nominating system under which they operate. Both because of the weaknesses in some of the rules and because voters in primaries have at times been shown to be questionable decision-makers, especially when there is a large number of candidates, I shall consider possible changes in the nominating system. In this chapter I shall offer a proposal for reforming the presidential selection system that should increase the chances that voters in primaries will make better choices.

THE QUALIFICATIONS OF VOTERS IN PRIMARIES

The results of the previous chapters question the validity of many of the criticisms of voters in primaries. First, the complaint that too few voters turn out in primaries appears unwarranted. While turnout is not as high as in general elections, registered party voters participate in larger numbers when a contest becomes important to the selection process, suggesting that voters are not apathetic, as implied by the lower rates of participation, but instead respond to the potential decisiveness of each primary. Second, contrary to conventional wisdom, electorates in primaries are not better paid, better educated, or more ideologically extreme than the party following. In fact, just the reverse is true, though the differences are small enough to have few consequences when selecting candidates. This finding is particularly important. If voters were more ideologically extreme than the party following, candidates lacking the necessary popular support to compete successfully in the general election may be more likely to gain the nomination than in a "representative" system. In addition, primaries should not prevent political parties from being responsive to mainstream America. Third, voters in primaries bring reasonable criteria to the polling booth, choosing candidates, for the most part, on the basis of personality traits. Since candidates from the same party often have few clear differences on matters of policy, it is certainly defensible for voters to consider a candidate's qualities of leadership and personal attributes. Fourth, voters in primaries may be better informed than many of their detractors suggest. Voters in primaries are as well informed as voters in presidential elections when two candidates compete for the nomination. Furthermore, voters become more informed as the primaries wear on, suggesting that one of the virtues of this nominating system is that it educates citizens about politics.

Even though voters in primaries are more qualified than many critics think, there are problems with them as presidential selectors. When there are a large number of aspirants, voters in primaries generally become familiar with only those candidates the news media consider "serious" contenders. The electorate, thus, fails to consider the full range of possible candidates. To compound matters, when there is a large field of candidates, some of the contenders who receive coverage are relatively unknown. For these less well known figures, voters appear to rely largely on the news media's portrayal of them since they have little prior information about them. Consequently, with a surge of positive coverage by the news media, a candidate can quickly become a front-runner, as was the case with Jimmy Carter and Gary Hart. If a relatively unknown candidate gains some notoriety and then receives bad press, that contender will fade quickly from the scene. George Bush's decline in the polls after the 1980 New Hampshire primary is an example of this pattern. Finally, without any coverage by the news media, an unknown candidate is doomed to failure. Because contests for the nomination are often multicandidate affairs, this weakness of voters in primaries raises doubts about their capacity to select nominees wisely.

There are additional problems with the current system not related to the capacity of voters in primaries to choose good candidates. Given the long series of primary battles, the initial contests, particularly in New Hampshire and Iowa, assume a great deal of influence in the process. In 1984, for example, the results in Iowa and New Hampshire brought Gary Hart to the front of the pack while they doomed the candidacies of John Glenn and Alan Cranston, among others. In fact, since 1972, no candidate has won the nomination without winning at least one of these two contests. It is unfair to allow only 2 states so much influence because it denies partisans in the other 48 an equal say in the process.

Other rules governing primaries interfere with the ability of voters in primaries to make good choices. The current ballot, for instance, can help candidates with narrow but intense support defeat opponents who have broad appeal. In addition, some states limit participation to partisans only. In these cases the results of the primary may provide few indicators of how candidates fare among both core party voters and "swing" voters in general elections. Finally, most methods of allocating delegates to candidates inaccurately reflect the preferences of voters. These shortcomings increase the risk of nominating candidates who may only be popular with a minority of the electorate.

In short, there are a number of problems with the current system both because of the characteristics of voters in primaries and because of the rules that govern the system. Problems of this sort help explain why many political scientists want to reform the present system. When considering whether to alter the nominating system, there are three basic courses of action to be considered: further enlarging the role of voters in primaries, increasing the role of party leaders, or maintaining the present state of affairs.[1] The findings presented here suggest that some change is necessary. The question becomes, then, whether party leaders or voters in primaries should be given more influence in the selection process.

SHOULD WE INCREASE THE ROLE OF PARTY LEADERS?

The weaknesses of the current system, whether perceived or real, have led some scholars to call for greater influence for party leaders (Ceasar 1982; Davis 1983; Polsby 1983). A greater role for party leaders in the selection of candidates will allow, these proponents argue, for "deliberation" and "peer review"—two qualities, they contend, absent from the present system.[2] Ranney describes the importance of peer review:

The absence of peer review means that the candidates are chosen by people who know them only as fakes on television and as personalities described by the news media; they are not chosen by people who know them personally and who have worked with them in situations of stress that show a person's true leadership qualities. Candidates are strangers chosen by strangers, not peers reviewed by peers. (see Ceasar 1982, p. 96)

"Deliberation," on the other hand, is a way to consider a large number of candidates for the nomination, weighing carefully their relative merits. Polsby (1983), for instance, argues that deliberation is a "criterion by which a choice process is evaluated to mean, simply, that the devices for aggregating individual preferences into collective choices maintain some capacity for receiving, manipulating and responding to a wider range of information than the first choice of participants'' (p. 171).

In other words, party leaders have information that voters in primaries do not possess. This information should allow party leaders to avoid some of the problems facing voters in primaries. With more information about the candidates, party leaders are more independent of the news media's portrayal of the contenders. Moreover, a large field of candidates does not pose as great a problem as when voters choose, because party leaders have information about all the contending candidates. In short, party leaders can choose popular candidates under conditions in which voters in primaries have a much more difficult time doing so.

While there are good reasons for allowing party leaders to choose candidates, the present nominating system does not give them a major role in the selection of nominees. The question becomes then whether the nominating system should be reformed to increase the role of party leaders in the selection process. To begin with, parties should *not* rely on party leaders as the final arbiters in choosing candidates as they did in the "mixed" system. Any attempt to curtail significantly the public's role in the process would bring a strong negative reaction from the news media and other interested groups, since they would surely see such a move as antidemocratic. But just as important, such a restoration may not be desirable. Party leaders have at times picked weak candidates just as voters in primaries have. It is by no means clear which selector has the less tarnished record.[3] We need to avoid being nostalgic about the convention system. Recall the many criticisms leveled against party leaders noted in the first chapter. So even if giving party leaders control over the process were possible, there are reasons not to do so.

There are, nonetheless, ways to integrate local, state, and national politicians in the selection process while maintaining an important role for the rank and file.[4] The Democrats in 1984 and 1988, for example, tried to increase "peer review" in the process by setting aside a proportion of seats for party officials. Walter Mondale in fact had to rely on these at-large delegates to assure a first-ballot victory over Gary Hart. The actual influence of these delegates depends heavily, of course, on what proportion of the total delegates they constitute and the closeness of the contest. In situations like 1984, they are likely to play a pivotal role since they can provide the margin of victory. While the prospect of securing these delegates would encourage candidates to contact party leaders and give party leaders a greater voice, simply increasing the number of at-large delegates would not solve the ills of the present system. Primaries would still operate under many of the same rules, New Hampshire would retain its position, and multicandidate races would still pose the same problems for the electorate. I shall propose, instead, a plan that would introduce major reforms into the system and allow both the party leaders and the rank and file of each party an effective voice in the process.

The proposal I describe below rests on two assumptions. First, primaries are here to stay. Scholars and political observers may not like these devices, but it seems unlikely that any effort to reestablish the old brokered conventions would work. Over the course of American history the nominating process has continued to be more democratized. It is unlikely one can put the brakes on this long-term trend. The second assumption is that the nominating system should be structured to select candidates with widespread support. This latter assumption rests on my belief that the fundamental purpose of political parties is to win elections. The selection process should, therefore, be able to choose candidates whom the electorate is willing to support in November.

A PROPOSAL FOR REFORM

A nominating system of grouped primaries offers a better way to select presidential nominees than currently exists.[5] This system would have, in effect, five Super Tuesdays. These contests should be separated by three weeks or so, allowing enough time for voters to digest the results and for contenders to adjust their strategies. The last group will be followed by a national convention that would formally nominate the presidential ticket.

While a proposal for a grouped system of primaries is not new,[6] my system has a number of new and important features. Each group of primaries would be created so that its members would have roughly the same ideological composition. A group like that in the first Super Tuesday of the 1984 contest, when three relatively conservative southern states and two primarily liberal New England states held primaries,[7] serves as a rough idea of what I have in mind. It is not easy, of course, to create an "ideologically" balanced series of primaries, because determining which states are liberal and which are conservative is extremely difficult. Fortunately, there have been two recent efforts to measure a state's ideological ranking (Rosenstone 1983; Bartels 1983). These rankings provide a way to generate ideologically balanced groups.

In addition to ideological balancing, there are other considerations that should enter into any grouping of states. Each group should have similar amounts of delegates at stake; the states should be as contiguous as possible; each group should encompass the major media markets of that cluster; and the major demographic characteristics should be balanced. Making the groups as contiguous as possible and maintaining the major media markets within each group should help lessen campaign costs and travel time for the candidates. Furthermore, by balancing the delegate

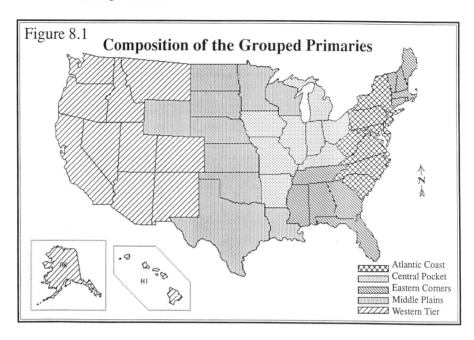

Figure 8.1

Composition of the Grouped Primaries

Atlantic Coast
Central Pocket
Eastern Corners
Middle Plains
Western Tier

totals and the demographics of the states, the groups will be made even more "equal" than if I just relied on ideological balance. Using measures for all these criteria, Figure 8.1 presents one possible plan for grouping states.[8] As one can see, this scheme is similar to some regional plans, except that the South and New England are placed together so as to balance the ideological leanings of these two areas.[9]

There are four additional rules governing the operation of these grouped primaries. First, each contest will employ the preference ballot rather than plurality voting. Second, any registered voter can participate in these contests who is willing to declare publicly that he or she is a partisan of the party. Third, 25 percent of the delegates will be set aside for party leaders. Fourth, delegates will be allocated by proportional representation schemes, with some minimum share of the vote necessary before one can receive any delegates.

There are a number of advantages to this system. First, relying on ideologically balanced groups of primaries minimizes potential biases that occur under regional plans or even under the current arrangement. A regional scheme, for example, would introduce ideological biases because the regions of this country vary in ideological makeup. If the first group of contests was held in the south, a candidate like Al Gore would have an edge over a Dukakis or a Simon. But if groups of states were ideologically balanced, these problems should be lessened.

Second, with a number of contests held at one time, it will be harder for the news media to determine a single "winner." With a single contest it is easier to judge winners and losers, but with a large number of contests at once there is a strong likelihood that there will be a split decision. While the news media will surely try to declare a winner, their interpretations will be more cautious (Arterton 1984). After the first Super Tuesday in the 1984 Democratic race, when Hart won three of five primaries and Mondale won the crucial state of Georgia, the news media saw *both* Hart and Mondale as winners.[10] If, however, one candidate wins nearly all the contests, that contender deserves the status of "winner." George Bush, for instance, received such coverage after his near sweep of the 1988 Super Tuesday contests. Finally, when the news media report "winners" and "losers," their interpretations will be based on more contests than just the results of one or two states. Under the current state of affairs, New Hampshire and Iowa play this role of creating winners and losers. The news media will still be in a "rush," as Arterton (1978) argues, to make assessments under my arrangement, but their coverage will be based on better tests of the electoral strengths of the candidates.

Another major advantage of a grouped system is that fewer unknown candidates would compete. Since a candidate would have to have a large organization to compete in many states at once, only contenders with substantial financial backing (and probably some name recognition) could realistically run. By contrast, with Iowa and New Hampshire being the first contests, a candidate can operate a small organization and hope to parlay support in these two contests into money, volunteers, and coverage by the news media for subsequent contests. But such small-scale organizations will be less effective in a grouped system.[11] With better-known and better-financed candidates running, more voters will be better able to consider the entire field than under the present state of affairs. The news media's coverage of the first contests, then, would no longer be the primary source of information for voters about the contenders, lessening the news media's influence. Moreover, with fewer candidates, the news media's "strategic" decisions over who to cover would not loom so large. Finally, better-known candidates are likely to have more experience in government since their name recognition suggests some previous accomplishments in public life. With greater experience, the contenders, on average, should be better campaigners and perhaps more effective presidents once elected. In short, this grouped system should eliminate important weaknesses of the current system.

Under this proposal, turnout should also increase since more contests are likely to be seen as important. As Chapter 3 showed, the more important a contest, the greater the participation. Since each group of states will be critical to the prospects of all contenders, there should be greater interest in each one. In the current system, later primaries may not be important in selecting candidates, which appears to depress turnout. With fewer election days, the last set of contests is more likely to be an important test for the candidates than they are at present. Some individual states within each group may be seen as more crucial than others, but on the whole, more primaries should be seen as important, which should increase the overall rate of participation.

The process will also take less time, which has some additional advantages. A shorter time-span should lessen the "excessive expenditure of money, time, and energy" that occurs under the present arrangement (Polsby 1983, p. 173). Anthony King (1981), for example, contends that "the length of the American nominating process and its grueling character undoubtedly have the effect of causing many able men and women to eliminate themselves from the race before it has even begun" (p. 321). So, perhaps the quality of candidates will increase. Of course, as Stephen Hess (1988) notes, the long process can provide a useful test of a candidate's ability to withstand pressure. While this reformed system will not be as long as the current process, it still should provide some insight into a candidate's ability to respond to pressure.

Another advantage of this system is its efforts to integrate party leaders into the process. One-quarter of the delegates should be set aside for party leaders such as members of Congress, governors, state legislators, and other party officials. With 25 percent of delegate slots given to party leaders, candidates would have to court these leaders for their support, which should help generate peer review and help establish contacts that should prove useful if elected. These delegates would be very important in a close contest, giving party leaders an important deciding voice. I chose 25 percent as the cutoff because a candidate would need 67 percent of elected delegates to gain the nomination if all party leaders were opposed to his or her nomination. If a candidate receives such support in the primaries, party leaders should not be allowed to block the nomination. But such large support is unlikely, which makes it important for any candidate to seek the support of local, state, and national party officials. This proportion of delegates does not, however, give party leaders veto power, because they too would be under pressure to support the "winner" of the primaries. In addition, party leaders are unlikely to be united behind one candidate, which splits their votes and hence diminishes their influence.

There are three aspects of this proposal that should maximize the chances that the candidate winning the most delegates would also be a strong contender in the November election. The first is the preference ballot. Primaries are criticized for not being able to show voters' second and third preferences. Ranney (1978) argues that:

A primary, like a referendum, is a device for registering and counting already formed first preferences. It has no way of identifying, let alone aggregating, second and third choices so as to discover the candidate with the broadest—as opposed to the most intense—support. And since broad support is much better than narrow but intensive support for unifying the party (nation) and appealing to the general electorate, this is a serious deficiency. (pp. 20–21)

By adopting the preference ballot, the new system will avoid this problem. Second, all delegates chosen in primaries will be allocated proportionally to candidates to ensure that delegate totals are commensurate with their electoral strength.[12] The third change would be to allow independents and potential defectors from the other party to participate in the process, providing they declare their partisanship publicly. Since raiding does not appear to be a major problem, participation by these swing voters can allow the selection system to get a better measure of how potential candidates would fare in the general election.

A final advantage of my proposal is that the national convention remains the official mechanism for selecting the nominee. The convention provides a rallying point for the party, a chance to heal wounds, a forum to write a party platform, and an opportunity for the 50 states to organize for a national campaign (Davis 1983). So, while the convention may come too late in the process to have a major voice in the actual choice of a nominee, it still serves a number of useful purposes.

This proposal alleviates many of the problems of the current system. It discourages unknown candidates with little financial backing from running, which decreases the news media's influence since voters are more likely to know more of the candidates prior to the campaign. One might argue, however, that given this desire to lessen the influence of the news media and to increase the information of voters, a one-day national primary may make even more sense. Under such a system only the best-known candidates could compete successfully. Moreover, the news media would pay a lot of attention to a national primary, which should increase voters' interest and information. Perhaps for these reasons, many observers of American politics have advocated a nationwide primary.[13]

This proposal, however, while having some benefits of the grouped system, introduces additional costs that make it undesirable. First, the news media would play a critical role in this system—perhaps larger than in the current system. With only one contest, the news media's decisions about who were "serious" candidates would be critical in determining which contenders the voters would consider. Moreover, it would be very difficult to get the news media to change their assessments. In the current system the results from the early primaries can affect the news media's coverage. In 1984 probably only Mondale and Glenn would have been considered serious candidates. There would have been little opportunity for candidates like Gary Hart to generate support in behalf of their candidacies. While my proposal also lessens the chances of less well known candidates (when compared to the current arrangement), such contenders would have an opportunity to build support in the electorate providing they raised sufficient money to campaign in the initial group of primaries. Since only 20 percent or so of the delegates are elected on the first day, the nomination is far from over. So my plan falls somewhere in between the current arrangement and a one-day national primary, providing the less well known some prospect of victory.

A second problem with a one-day national primary is that one massive contest would prevent any candidate from building momentum and support for the general-election campaign. If a candidate wins 51 percent of the vote nationwide while a runner-up receives the other 49 percent, the former wins the nomination. Yet in such a close contest it might be hard for the party to present a unified effort in the November election. A loss by 2 percentage points may leave bitter feelings on both sides. Under my system a candidate could generate a wave of support and enthusiasm that could spill over into the general election. Moreover, the convention, which often serves as a rallying point for the general election, would lose importance, since the one-day primary would select the nominee. Whatever wounds that exist from that primary would, therefore, have little opportunity to heal.

Another important problem with a national direct primary is that party leaders would have little say in the process. The winner of the national primary, regardless of the closeness of the race, becomes the nominee. A candidate would not need the support of party leaders to win—though, of course, their support would help a candidate's cause. Consequently, peer review, as Polsby and Ranney define it, would be a thing of the past.

As one can see, a national primary introduces a number of potentially serious problems. The system I propose is certainly not without flaw, but the arrangement offers a way to give both party leaders and the rank and file an important voice in the process. And at the same time, the particular rules take advantage of the strengths of voters while minimizing the weaknesses.

FINAL OBSERVATIONS

When the Founding Fathers met in 1787 to write the Constitution, they were faced with a question similar to the one that now confronts legislators and party leaders: Who would serve as the best presidential selectors? The Founders considered whether to allow the electorate to select the president directly or to have the national legislature choose the chief executive (Wilmerding 1958).[14] The Founders decided after much debate to compromise, establishing the electoral college—an independent body of electors.[15] The current choice is whether to rely on the rank and file or the party leaders to nominate candidates. There is an inevitable conflict between these two sets of decision-makers because if one gains power, the other loses it. For about 140 years party leaders had the last word on who would be the nominee. But with the recent proliferation of primaries, the rank and file assumed that role. Many scholars have claimed that the electorate is not capable of making such decisions, just as many of the Founders claimed over 200 years ago. This study, however, has questioned the validity of many of their complaints.

These findings, however, do not mean that voters in primaries should be given complete power in the selection of candidates. As shown by the problems created when large numbers of unknown candidates compete, party leaders should be given a say in the process because they are better informed than the rank and file and are not as vulnerable to news media's coverage of the candidates. The proposal I present attempts to provide a balance between these two decision-makers. This grouped system does not end the tension but provides a way for both groups to influence the choice of candidates. If there is a popular candidate, that contender should be able to win in the system I propose. But if there is no clear popular choice, party leaders will have the discretion to make the decision.

One can obviously quarrel with part or all of this plan. The more important issue, however, concerns one's assessment of voters in presidential primaries. History has demonstrated that those who possess most of the responsibility for choosing nominees will come under attack. The problem is that these attacks were (and are) often made without sufficient evidence and without clearly establishing the criteria for defining good decision-makers. This study has sought to overcome these problems by presenting data about the qualifications of voters in primaries and explicit discussions of what those qualifications should be.

In general, the findings presented here shift the focus of debate concerning the current nominating system, because no longer can one call for reform by simply arguing that voters in presidential primaries are unrepresentative, uninterested and uninformed. But as noted above, these results do not mean that voters in presidential primaries are "qualified" to choose presidential nominees. The evidence presented here provides some support for these decision-makers, but it is clear that some serious weaknesses arise when voters in primaries select nominees. Because of these problems some changes must be made in the system. I have made one set of recommendations.

Whether one agrees with these recommendations or my evaluation of voters in primaries, this debate about their qualifications to choose presidential nominees is far from over. Scholars will continue to collect data about voters in primaries, providing additional insights into these decision-makers. Given that voters in primaries have selected only a handful of candidates, additional data are necessary to refine and modify the generalizations about these participants. In addition, political scientists will develop alternative standards to judge the qualifications of voters, which should shed further light on their merits as decision-makers. But perhaps most important, this debate will continue because the nominating process is a coveted source of power in the American political arena. And because of its importance, one can expect this struggle to continue over who, as Boss Tweed once said, gets to "do the nominating."

NOTES

1. Ceasar (1982) makes a similar three-prong classification concerning possible courses for reform, labeling them 1. "more direct democracy," 2. "rationalizing the status quo," and 3. "increasing the role of representative decision-making."

2. Actually, "peer review" occurs under the present arrangement; it just takes place in the early stages of the selection process. A candidate generally becomes a serious contender—one able to command money and media attention—when the party leadership considers this individual a good choice. Mondale's status as the front-runner in 1984 is an example of just such an effect. Mondale was viewed as the likely nominee not just because voters and the news media were actively supporting his selection after the 1980 election, but rather, Mondale's status as a front-runner was, in part, because political elites felt he was the best choice available, especially once Senator Kennedy withdrew from the race. Their assessment led them to endorse his candidacy and help raise funds for his prenomination campaign. Michael Hawthorne (1984) provides evidence of "peer review" in the current system, showing that prenomination campaigns establish "links with local politicians and activists, though not necessarily through the party, but instead through candidate organization and personal networks. This is not the role which individuals like Schattschneider would prefer the party to play, but it does establish a link between nomination campaigns and other elected and party officials. It is informal, and may or may not withstand the election and survive after taking office. But to suggest that presidential nomination campaigns operate without linkages to others in the political system may be vastly overstating the situation" (pp. 18–19).

3. There are, of course, measures of presidential greatness, which can provide insights into the quality of candidates chosen by a nominating system. Kenney and Rice (1988) present one set of rankings from the *Chicago Tribune*. According to those data, the average ranking of presidents selected under the "mixed" system was 17. The scale runs from 1 to 37, suggesting that a 17 is about average. This number seems reasonable. While FDR, Truman, and Wilson are generally viewed as very good presidents, the mixed system also selected Harding, Coolidge, and Nixon. Thus it seems that the previous system had a checkered record of presidential selection, as suggested above.

It is hard to compare these numbers to those in the current system. Carter ranked 26th, a poor showing. Reagan, on the other hand, is likely to be placed high on this scale. Kenney and Rice (1988) predict a ranking of about 13th over-all. But with just two cases, few conclusions can be made.

4. Polsby (1983) provides a thoughtful account of possible avenues of reform. While he rejects a rebirth of the national convention because it comes too late in the process to choose candidates, he offers a number of possible courses of action, such as increasing the number of at-large delegates, electing unbound delegates, and shortening the time between the first and last prenomination contests (see Chapter 5). Ceasar (1982) also discusses various options for change.

5. In this proposal, states can only use primaries to select delegates. One could argue that caucuses should also be allowed in this system. I have no quarrel with this option. But since I have focused on primaries in this book and have presented little evidence about caucuses, I have limited my attention to primaries.

6. Senator Robert Packwood's proposal for grouping primaries by region is perhaps the best-known plan.

7. Also, four caucuses were held on Super Tuesday in Hawaii, Oklahoma, Nevada, and Washington.

8. This grouping plan was originally developed by Stephen Dunne (1984); his work *only* involves the grouping scheme, not the other aspects of this proposal. His paper provides the details about how this system was created.

9. One might argue with the exact location of some of the states, seeking to revise this particular plan. Such changes would be welcome. My objective is not to offer this scheme as the only acceptable plan. My major purpose is instead to propose a system of grouped primaries that meets the five criteria listed above. Other plans may accomplish those goals as well. But the Dunne proposal has much merit.

10. Tom Brokaw of NBC News, commenting on the Super Tuesday results, said "Walter Mondale: alive and well tonight in the race for the Democratic nomination," and then went on to state that Gary Hart "emerges from this day, if not superman, at least with a lot of additional muscle tonight." Dan Rather of CBS News also gave positive reviews to both candidates: "The overview is that the candidacy of Senator Gary Hart of Colorado keeps moving like a fast freight, the candidacy of Walter Mondale is off the side rails, and moving forward again. . . ."

In the *New York Times*, March 14th, 1984, the front-page headline read:

HART TAKES MASSACHUSETTS
FLORIDA AND RHODE ISLAND;
MONDALE IS STRONG IN SOUTH

The *Washington Post* reconfirms this pattern:

HART WINS 3, MONDALE 2;
MCGOVERN QUITS RACE

11. It is possible, however, that a poorly funded contender could concentrate on just one state and try to translate a good showing into greater support in future contests. Such efforts would be risky since nearly 20 percent of the delegates would have been selected by the time that person's campaign had gotten off the ground.

12. Recall that in instances where no candidate receives 50 percent of first-preference votes, the preference ballot shuffles the vote until one candidate receives 50 percent of the electorates' support. At that point delegates are allocated proportionally to the *remaining* candidates (see Chapter 7).

13. There have been over 250 proposals for a direct national primary since Woodrow Wilson first introduced such a plan to Congress in 1913. The public also supports such a plan. In a June 1984 survey, 67 percent of respondents in a Gallup poll favored adopting a national direct primary. See Martin Wattenberg (1984) and William Crotty and John Jackson (1985) for descriptions of possible plans.

14. Many of the Founders feared the direct election of the chief executive. They thought the mass electorate would be likely to make bad choices because such a choice was too difficult for the average voter to undertake—see, for instance, Max Farrand (1937) and Lucius Wilmerding (1958).

Many Founders also feared that an institutionalized assembly, such as a legislature, would ignore the wishes of the electorate and encourage the corruption of the president. Gouverneur Morris argued, for example, that if the legislature chose the president he "would be the mere creature of the legislature"; his election would be the "work of intrigue, of cabal, and of faction; it will be like the election of a pope by a conclave of cardinals; real merit will rarely be the title to appointment." Morris quoted from John Kasson (1904, p. 102).

15. As Alexander Hamilton argued in *The Federalist*, no. 68, the members of the electoral college would have the needed expertise, because a "small number of persons, selected by their fellow citizens from the general mass, will be the most likely to possess the information and discernment requisite to so complicated an investigation." In short, the electoral college did not "depend on any preexisting bodies of men, who might be tampered with beforehand to prostitute their votes" (*The Federalist*, no. 68).

Appendix I

Definition of Variables Used in Explaining Turnout

1. Turnout: The data on turnout were arrived at by dividing the number of citizens who voted in a primary by the number of registered party voters in that state. The data on the number of voters are from *Presidential Elections Since 1796*, 3d and 4th editions, published by Congressional Quarterly. Data on registered party voters are from Ranney (1977), *The Republican Almanac*, published by the Republican National Committee, and Rhodes Cook (1987) *Race for the Presidency*, published by Congressional Quarterly.

2. Education: These data are the proportion of citizens in each state who completed at least four years of high school. The source is the *Statistical Abstract of the United States*, published by the Bureau of the Census.

3. Media Attention: Aldrich (1980) ranks the news media coverage of the states for 1976 (see his Appendix, Table 13). Robinson and Sheehan (1983) provide information on the CBS and UPI coverage of the primaries for 1980 (see pp. 176–77). I take the 1980 data and rank the states by amount of media coverage, as Aldrich (1980) did. The variable ranges from a value of 1, the least covered, to 15, the most covered.

4. Campaign Spending: Campaign spending is measured by dividing the dollars spent by all candidates in a party's primary by the number of registered party voters in that state, then taking the logs of this measure. The logged value is a much stronger explanatory variable than the linear value, because campaign spending brings diminishing returns. Money is very important at the outset, but once a candidate's name is known, additional funds have less and less effect. Data on spending are from the *Federal Election Commission*.

5. Competitiveness: Competitiveness is arrived at by subtracting the proportion of the vote for the first-place candidate from that for the second-place candidate. This value is then subtracted from 100. This formula is used for the actual outcome in primaries and the delegate totals of the candidates. For data on the closeness of individual races I used *Presidential Elections Since 1796*, 3rd edition. For data on delegate totals in each year, I used the *Congressional Quarterly Weekly Report*.

6. Date of the Primary: The date of the contest is the number of weeks that have passed since the first primary was held. Thus, New Hampshire is 0, while Massachusetts in 1976 and 1980 is 1.

7. Old and New Primaries: If a primary was not held in the previous nomination contest for that state, then the primary was deemed to be "new."

Appendix II

Description of Survey Questions

Libcon	R's (respondent's) position on the liberal-conservative scale
Def-Sp.	R's position on defense spending
Gov-Sp.	R's position on government spending
Russia	R's position on relations with the USSR
Infla.	R's position on the tradeoff between inflation and unemployment
Aid-Min	R's position on aid to minorities
Central America	R's position on the U.S. role in Central America
Gov-Job	R's position on whether government should provide jobs
Busing	R's position on whether busing should be used to integrate schools
Med-Ins	R's position on medical insurance
Abort	R's position on abortion
Women	R's position on women's rights

Question Wording for Patterson's Panel Study

[Welfare]: There is a lot of talk these days about the level of spending by the federal government for social welfare programs. Some people feel that the current level of social welfare spending is necessary because almost everyone receiving this government help really needs it. Others feel a great deal of this social welfare spending is wasted because a lot of people receiving this government help don't deserve it. Which number on the scale below would best describe your feelings on this issue, or haven't you thought much about it? Where would you place (candidate) on this scale, or don't you know about his position?

[Busing]: Some people think achieving racial integration of schools is so important that it justifies busing children to schools out of their own neighborhoods. Others think letting children go to their neighborhood schools is so important that they oppose busing. Which number on the scale would best describe your feelings on this issue, or haven't you thought much about it? Where would you place (candidate) on this scale, or don't you know about his position?

[Tax Cut]: Most everyone favors a cut in personal income taxes, but there is disagreement about the nature of the tax cut. Some people want a tax cut that is intended to benefit all income groups about the same. Other people want a tax cut that is intended to benefit modest and low-income groups much more than it benefits high-income groups. Which number on the scale would best describe your feelings on this issue, or haven't you thought much about it? Where would you place (candidate) on this scale, or don't you know about his position?

[Abortion]: Some people favor legalized abortion, that is, they feel a woman who desires an abortion should be able to have one. Other people are against legalized abortion. Which number on the scale best describes your feelings on this issue, or haven't you thought much about it? Where would you place (candidate) on this scale, or don't you know about his position?

[Defense]: Some people think our military strength has diminished in comparison to Russia's and that much more must be spent on planes, ships, and weapons to build a stronger defense. Others feel that our military defense is adequate and that no increase in military spending is currently necessary. Which number on the scale best describes your feelings on this issue, or haven't you thought much about it? Where would you place (candidate) on this scale, or don't you know about his position?

[Gov't Jobs]: As a way to reduce unemployment, most people feel the government should help business to prosper so that more jobs are created. But people have different opinions about the government directly providing jobs. Some people want a federal job program, where the government *directly* provides jobs to those who cannot otherwise find employment. Others do not want the government *directly* to provide jobs to those out of work. Which number on the scale best describes your feelings on this issue, or haven't you thought much about it? Where would you place (candidate) on this scale, or don't you know about his position?

Question Wording for 1980 NES panel study

[Defense]: Some people believe that we should spend much less money for defense. Suppose these people are at one end of the scale at point number 1. Others feel that defense spending should be greatly increased. Suppose these people are at the other end, at point 7. And, of course, some other people have opinions somewhere in between at points 2, 3, 4, 5, or 6. Where would you place yourself on this scale, or haven't you thought much about this? Where would you place (candidate) on this scale?

[Aid to Min]: Some people feel that the government in Washington should make every possible effort to improve the social and economic position of blacks and other minority groups, even if it means giving them preferential treatment. (Suppose these people are at one end of the scale at point number 1.) Others feel that the government should not make any special effort to help minorities because they should help themselves. (Suppose these people are at the other end, at point 7. And, of course, some other people have opinions somewhere in between at points 2, 3, 4, 5, or 6). Where would you place yourself on this scale, or haven't you thought much about this? Where would you place (candidate) on this scale?

[Gov't Service]: Some people think the government should provide fewer services in areas such as health and education, in order to reduce spending. Other people feel it is important for government to continue the services it now provides even if it means no reduction in spending. Where would you place yourself on this scale, or haven't you thought much about this? Where would you place (candidate) on this scale?

[U.S.S.R.]: Some people feel it is very important for us to try very hard to get along with Russia. Others feel it is a big mistake to try too hard to get along with Russia. Where would you place yourself on this scale, or haven't you thought much about this? Where would you place (candidate) on this scale?

[Unemp-infla]: Some people feel the federal government should take action to reduce the inflation rate, even if it means that unemployment would go up a lot. Others feel the government should take action to reduce the rate of unemployment, even if it means that inflation would go up a lot. Where would you place yourself on this scale, or haven't you thought much about this? Where would you place (candidate) on this scale?

Appendix III

The Coding of the Open-Ended Comments

Below is the coding scheme for the questions "What is the reason you favor (this candidate) over some other candidate?" and "What's the main reason you voted for that candidate?" Each respondent could make up to four comments for each question. Under the codes are a sample of responses. For a complete list of the open-ended responses see the codebook for the Patterson study (ICPSR #7990).

Issues: 005, 006, 008, 009, 100 to 153, 810, 811, 821, 870 to 891.

"I like his position on foreign affairs"

"He will help the economy"

"He supported busing"

Candidate characteristics: 001, 002, 003, 007, 010 to 080, 190 to 199, 200 to 405, 408, 409, 615, 616, 700, 701, 801 to 808, 819, 820, 829, 830, 840 to 849.

"He is well-qualified"

"He is a political newcomer, a fresh face"

"He is a good leader"

"His opponent has a poor personality"

Ideology: 406, 407, 410 to 414, 419, 860 to 863.

"He is a liberal"

"He is a moderate"

"His opponent is too conservative"

Group References: 160 to 181, 550 to 599.

"He is for the poor"

"He is for the working class"

"He is against the rich"

"He has a pro-labor record"

Campaign: 600 to 699, 850 to 859.

"He has a good chance of winning"

"He is a good campaigner"

"He will unite the party"

Other: 702, 800, 822, 899, 995, 996.

"He was not my first choice"

"He is from my state"

"I didn't have a choice"

Don't Know: 998

Bibliography

Abramowitz, Alan I. 1978. The Impact of a Presidential Debate on Voter Rationality. *American Journal of Political Science* 22:680–90.

———. 1987. Candidate Choice Before the Convention. *Political Behavior* 9:49–61.

———, and Walter Stone. 1984. *Nomination Politics: Party Activists and Presidential Choice*. New York: Praeger.

Adamany, David. 1976. Crossover Voting and the Democratic Party's Reform Rules. *American Political Science Review* 70:536–541.

Adams, William C. 1987. As New Hampshire Goes . . . In *Media and Momentum*, edited by Gary R. Orren and Nelson W. Polsby. Chatham, N.J.: Chatham House.

Aldrich, John. 1980. *Before the Convention*. Chicago: University of Chicago Press.

Arterton, F. Christopher. 1978. The Media Politics of Presidential Campaigns: A Study of the Carter Nomination Drive. In *Race for the Presidency*, edited by James D. Barber. Englewood Cliffs, N.J.: Prentice-Hall.

———. 1984. *Media Politics*. Lexington, Mass.: Lexington Books.

Asher, Herbert B. 1988. *Presidential Elections and American Politics*. 4th ed. Chicago: Dorsey Press.

Bartels, Larry M. 1983. Presidential Primaries and the Dynamics of Public Choice. Ph.D. diss., University of California, Berkeley.

———. 1985. Expectations and Preferences in Presidential Nominating Campaigns. *American Political Science Review* 79:812.

———. 1987. Candidate Choice and the Dynamics of the Presidential Nominating Process. *American Journal of Political Science* 31:1–31.

———. 1988. *Presidential Primaries and the Dynamics of Public Choice*. Princeton: Princeton University Press.

Black, Duncan. 1958. *The Theory of Committees and Elections.* Cambridge: Cambridge University Press.

Bode, Kenneth A., and Carol F. Casey. 1980. Party Reform: Revisionism Revisited. In *Political Parties in the Eighties*, edited by Robert A. Goldwin. Washington: American Enterprise Institute.

Brady, Henry E. 1984. Media and Momentum. Occasional Paper No. 85–7, Harvard University.

————, and Richard Johnston. 1987. What's the Primary Message: Horse Race or Issue Journalism? In *Media and Momentum*, edited by Gary R. Orren and Nelson W. Polsby. Chatham, N.J.: Chatham House.

Brams, Steven J. 1978. *The Presidential Election Game.* New Haven: Yale University Press.

————, and Peter C. Fishburn. 1983. *Approval Voting.* Boston: Birkhauser.

Bryce, James. 1891. *The American Commonwealth, Volume II.* 2d ed. New York: Macmillan and Co.

Campbell, Angus. 1960. Surge and Decline: The Study of Electoral Change. *Public Opinion Quarterly* 24:397–418.

————, Philip E. Converse, Warren E. Miller, and Donald E. Stokes. 1960. *The American Voter.* New York: Wiley.

Carleton, William G. 1953. The Collapse of the Caucus. *Current History* 25:144–51.

Ceasar, James W. 1979. *Presidential Selection: Theory and Development.* Princeton: Princeton University Press.

————. 1982. Reforming the Reforms. Cambridge, Mass.: Ballinger.

Chase, James. 1973. *Emergence of the Presidential Nominating Convention.* Urbana: University of Illinois Press.

Collat, Donald S., Stanley Kelley, Jr., and Ronald Rogowski. 1981. The End Game in Presidential Nominations. *American Political Science Review* 75:426–35.

Conover, Pamela J., and Stanley Feldman. 1981. The Origins and Meaning of Liberal/Conservative Self-Identification. *American Journal of Political Science* 25:617–45.

Converse, Philip E. 1964. The Nature of Belief Systems in Mass Publics. In *Ideology and Discontent*, edited by David E. Apter. New York: The Free Press.

————. 1974. Comment. *American Political Science Review* 68:1024–27.

Crotty, William J. 1977. *Political Reform and the American Experiment.* New York: Thomas Y. Crowell.

————. 1983. *Party Reform.* New York: Longman.

————, and John S. Jackson III. 1985. *Presidential Primaries and Nominations.* Washington, D.C.: Congressional Quarterly Press.

Crouse, Timothy. 1973. *The Boys on the Bus.* New York: Ballantine.

David, Paul T., and James W. Ceasar. 1980. *Proportional Representation in the Presidential Nominating Process.* Charlottesville: University Press of Virginia.

————, Ralph M. Goldman, and Richard C. Bain. 1960. *The Politics of National Party Conventions.* Washington, D.C.: Brookings Institution.

Davis, James W. 1980. *Presidential Primaries: Road to the White House.* Westport, Conn.: Greenwood Press.

————. 1983. *National Conventions in an Age of Party Reform.* Westport, Conn.: Greenwood Press.

DeMaio, Gerald, and Douglas Muzzio. 1981. The 1980 Elections and Approval Voting. *Presidential Studies Quarterly* 11:364–73.

DeNardo, James. 1988. The Strange Case of Surge and Decline. Paper presented at the annual meeting of the American Political Science Association, Washington, D.C.

DiNitto, Andrew, and William Smithers. 1972. The Representativeness of the Direct Primary: A Further Test of V. O. Key's Thesis. *Polity* 4:209–24.

Downs, Anthony. 1957. *An Economic Theory of Democracy.* New York: Harper & Row.

Dunne, Stephen. 1984. Grouped Primaries and Caucuses. Unpublished paper, Princeton University.

Epstein, Leon D. 1978. Political Science and Presidential Nominations. *Political Science Quarterly* 93:177–96.

Farley, James. 1940. *Behind the Ballots.* New York: Basic Books.

Farrand, Max. 1937. *Records of the Federal Conventions of 1787.* Rev. ed. New Haven: Yale University Press.

Gopoian, J. David. 1982. Issue Preferences and Candidate Choice in Presidential Primaries. *American Journal of Political Science* 26:523–46.

Graber, Doris. 1971. The Press as Opinion Resource During the 1968 Presidential Campaign. *Public Opinion Quarterly* 35:168–82.

————. 1972. Personal Qualities in Presidential Images: The Contribution of the Press. *Midwest Journal of Political Science* 16:46–76.

————. 1989. *Mass Media and American Politics.* 3d ed. Washington D.C.: Congressional Quarterly Press.

Hammond, Jack H. 1980. Another Look at the Role of "The Rules" in the 1972 Democratic Presidential Primaries. *Western Political Quarterly* 33:50–72.

Hawthorne, Michael R. 1984. Centralization and Decentralization in Presidential Nomination Campaigns. Paper presented at the annual meeting of the American Political Science Association, Washington, D.C.

Heale, M. J. 1982. *The Presidential Quest.* New York: Longman.

Hedlund, R. D. 1977–1978. Cross-over Voting in a 1976 Open Presidential Primary. *Public Opinion Quarterly* 41:498–514.

————, Meredith W. Watts, and David M. Hedge. 1982. Voting in an Open Primary. *American Politics Quarterly* 10:197–218.

Hess, Stephen. 1988. *The Presidential Campaign.* 3d ed. Washington, D.C.: The Brookings Institution.

Hoffman, David. 1988. Bush and Dole: A Campaign of Reflected Images. *Washington Post National Weekly Edition.* February 1–7:13.

Jacobson, Gary C. 1987. *The Politics of Congressional Elections.* 2d ed. Boston: Little, Brown & Co.

Jewell, Malcolm E. 1977. Turnout in State Gubernatorial Primaries. *Western Political Quarterly* 36:236–54.

Joslyn, Richard A. 1976. The Impact of Decision Rules in Multi-Candidate Campaigns: The Case of the 1972 Democratic Nomination. *Public Choice* 25:1–17.

———. 1984. *Mass Media and Elections*. Reading, Mass.: Addison-Wesley.

Kasson, John. 1904. *The Evolution of the Constitution of the United States*. Boston: Houghton Mifflin Co.

Keech, William R., and Donald R. Matthews. 1976. *The Party's Choice*. Washington, D.C.: The Brookings Institution.

Keeter, Scott, and Cliff Zukin. 1983. *Uninformed Choice*. New York: Praeger.

Kellet, John, and Kenneth Mott. 1977. Presidential Primaries: Measuring Popular Choice. *Polity* 9:528–37.

Kelley, Stanley, Jr. 1962. Mass Media and Elections. *Law and Contemporary Problems* 27:307–26.

———. 1983. *Interpreting Elections*. Princeton: Princeton University Press.

———, Richard Ayres, and William Bowen. 1967. Registration and Voting: Putting First Things First. *American Political Science Review* 61:359–79.

Kenney, Patrick J., and Tom W. Rice. 1985. Voter Turnout in Presidential Primaries. *Political Behavior* 7:101–12.

———. 1987a. A Model of Nomination Preferences. Paper presented at the annual meeting of the Southern Political Science Association, Charlotte, N.C.

———. 1987b. The Relationship between Divisive Primaries and General Election Outcomes. *American Journal of Political Science* 31:31–44.

———. 1988. Contextual Determinants of Presidential Greatness. *Presidential Studies Quarterly* 18:161–69.

Key, V. O. 1956. *American State Politics: An Introduction*. New York: Alfred A. Knopf.

———. 1964. *Politics, Parties, and Pressure Groups*. 5th ed. New York: Thomas Y. Crowell.

Kinder, Donald, and Robert Abelson. 1981. Appraising Presidential Candidates: Personality and Affect in the 1980 Campaign. Paper presented at the annual meeting of the American Political Science Association, New York City.

King, Anthony. 1981. How Not to Select Presidential Candidates: A View from Europe. In *The American Elections of 1980*, edited by Austin Ranney. Washington, D.C.: American Enterprise Institute.

Kirkpatrick, Jeane J. 1976. *The New Presidential Elite*. New York: Russell Sage Foundation.

———. 1978. *Dismantling the Parties: Reflections on Party Reform and Party Decline*. Washington, D.C.: American Enterprise Institute.

Kritzer, Herbert. 1977. The Representativeness of the 1972 Presidential Primaries. *Polity*, 10:121–29.

Ladd, Everett Carll, Jr. 1978. *Where Have All the Voters Gone?* New York: Norton.

Lakeman, Enid. 1970. *How Democracies Vote*. London: Faber and Faber.

Lengle, James I. 1981. *Representation and Presidential Primaries*. Westport, Conn.: Greenwood Press.

———, and Bryon E. Shafer. 1976. Primary Rules, Political Power, and Social Change. *American Political Science Review* 70:25–40.

Levy, Mark R. 1983. The Methodology and Performance of Election Day Polls. *Public Opinion Quarterly* 47:54–67.

Levitin, Teresa E., and Warren E. Miller. 1979. Ideological Interpretations of Presidential Elections. *American Political Science Review* 73:751–71.

Mann, Thomas. 1978. *Unsafe at Any Margin*. Washington, D.C.: American Enterprise Institute.

———, and Raymond Wolfinger. 1980. Candidates and Parties in Congressional Elections. *American Political Science Review* 74:617–32.

Marshall, Thomas R. 1981. *Presidential Nominations in a Reform Age*. New York: Praeger.

———. 1983. The News Verdict and Public Opinion During Presidential Primaries. In *Television Coverage of the 1980 Presidential Campaign*, edited by William C. Adams. Norwood, N.J.: Ablex.

———. 1984. Issues, Personalities and Presidential Primary Voters. *Social Science Quarterly* 65:750–60

Martin, Ralph G. 1964. *Ballots and Bandwagons*. Chicago: Rand McNally.

Markus, Gregory, and Philip Converse. 1979. A Dynamic Simultaneous Model of Electoral Choice. *American Political Science Review* 73:1055–70.

Matthews, Donald R. 1978. Winnowing. In *Race for the Presidency*, edited by James D. Barber. Englewood Cliffs, N.J.: Prentice-Hall.

McGovern, George, and Donald Frasier. 1970. *Commission on Party Structure and Delegate Selection, Mandate for Reform*. Washington, D.C.: Democratic National Committee.

Meyers, Ernst C. 1902. *Nominating Systems: Direct Primaries versus Conventions* Madison, Wisc.: Published by the author.

Miller, Warren E. 1988. *Without Consent*. Lexington, Ky.: The University Press of Kentucky.

———, and M. Kent Jennings. 1986. *Parties in Transition*. New York: Russell Sage Foundation.

Moore, David. 1984a. Myths of the New Hampshire Primary. Paper presented at the annual meeting of the American Political Science Association, Washington, D.C.

———. 1984b. The Death of Politics in New Hampshire. *Public Opinion* 7:56–57.

———, and Richard C. Hofstetter. 1973. The Representativeness of a Primary Election: Ohio. *Polity* 6:197–222.

Moran, Jack, and Mark Fenster. 1982. Voter Turnout in Presidential Primaries. *American Politics Quarterly* 10:453–76.

Mueller, Dennis. 1979. *Public Choice*. Cambridge: Cambridge University Press.

Nakamura, Robert A., and Denis G. Sullivan. 1978a. Neo-Conservatism and Presidential Nomination Reforms: A Critique. In *American Politics and Public Policy*, edited by Walter Dean Burnham and Martha W. Weinberg. Cambridge: MIT Press.

———. 1978b. Party Democracy and Democratic Control. In *American Politics and Public Policy*, edited by Walter Dean Burnham and Martha W. Weinberg. Cambridge: MIT Press.

Nelson, Michael. 1985. The Case for the Current Presidential Nominating Process. In *Before Nomination*, edited by George Grassmuck. Washington D.C.: American Enterprise Institute.

Nie, Norman, Sidney Verba, and John Petrocik. 1979. *The Changing American Voter* Cambridge: Harvard University Press.

Niemi, Richard G. 1984. The Problem of Strategic Behavior under Approval Voting. *American Political Science Review* 78:952–58.

―――, and Larry M. Bartels. 1984. The Responsiveness of Approval Voting to Political Circumstances. *PS* 17:571–76.

―――, and Herbert Weisberg. 1984. What Determines the Vote? In *Controversies in Voting Behavior*, edited by Richard G. Niemi and Herbert Weisberg. Washington, D.C.: Congressional Quarterly Press.

Norrander, Barbara. 1986a. Measuring Primary Turnout in Aggregate Analysis. *Political Behavior* 8:356–73.

―――. 1986b. Correlates of Vote Choice in the 1980 Presidential Primaries. *Journal of Politics* 48:156–66.

―――. 1989. Ideological Representativeness of Presidential Primary Voters. *American Journal of Political Science*, forthcoming.

―――, and Gregg W. Smith. 1985. Type of Contest, Candidate Strategy and Turnout in Presidential Primaries. *American Politics Quarterly* 13:28–50.

Orren, Gary R., and Nelson W. Polsby. 1987. New Hampshire: Springboard of Nomination Politics. In *Media and Momentum*, edited by Gary R. Orren and Nelson W. Polsby. Chatham, N.J.: Chatham House.

Ostrogorski, M. 1900. The Rise and Fall of the Nominating Caucus, Legislative and Congressional Caucuses. *American Historical Review* 5:253–83.

―――. 1921. *Democracy and the Party System*. New York: Macmillan.

Overacker, Louise. 1926. *The Presidential Primary*. New York: Macmillan.

Page, Benjamin I., and Calvin C. Jones. 1979. Reciprocal Effects of Policy Preferences, Party Loyalties and the Vote. *American Political Science Review* 73:1071–89.

Patterson, Thomas E. 1980. *The Mass Media Election*. New York: Praeger.

―――, and Robert D. McClure. 1976. *The Unseeing Eye*. New York: Putnam.

Polsby, Nelson W. 1960. Decision-Making at the National Conventions. *Western Political Quarterly* 13:609–19.

―――. 1980. The News Media as an Alternative to Party in the Presidential Selection Process. In *Political Parties in the 1980s*, edited by Robert A. Goldwin. Washington, D.C.: American Enterprise Institute.

―――. 1983. *Consequences of Party Reform*. New York: Oxford University Press.

―――, and Aaron Wildavsky. 1988. *Presidential Elections*. 7th ed. New York: The Free Press.

Pomper, Gerald. 1979. New Rules and New Games in Presidential Nominations. *Journal of Politics* 41:784–805.

Rae, Douglas. 1971. *The Political Consequences of Election Laws*. 2d ed. New Haven: Yale University Press.

Ranney, Austin. 1968. Representativeness of Primary Electorates. *Midwest Journal of Political Science* 12:224–38.

―――. 1972. Turnout and Representation in American Presidential Elections. *American Political Science Review* 66:21–37.

———. 1975. *Curing the Mischiefs of Faction: Party Reform in America*. Berkeley: University of California Press.

———. 1977. *Participation in American Presidential Nominations*. Washington, D.C.: American Enterprise Institute.

———. 1978. Changing the Rules of the Presidential Nominating Game. In *Parties and Elections*, edited by Jeff Fishel. Bloomington, Ind.: Indiana University Press.

———. 1983. *Channels of Power*. New York: Basic Books.

———, and Leon Epstein. 1966. The Two Electorates: Voters and Non-Voters in a Wisconsin Primary. *Journal of Politics* 28:598–616.

Reiter, Howard L. 1985. *Selecting the President*. Philadelphia: University of Pennsylvania Press.

Robinson, Michael S. 1978. TV's Newest Program: The "Presidential Nominations Game." *Public Opinion* 1:41–46.

———, and Margaret A. Sheehan. 1983. *Over the Wire and on TV*. New York: Russell Sage Foundation.

Rosenstone, Steven J. 1983. *Forecasting Presidential Elections*. New Haven: Yale University Press.

Rothenberg, Lawrence, and Richard A. Brody. 1988. Participation in Presidential Primaries. *Western Political Quarterly* 41: 253–72.

Rubin, Richard. 1980. Presidential Primaries: Continuities, Dimensions of Change, and Political Implications. In *The Party Symbol*, edited by William Crotty. San Francisco: W. H. Freeman.

Sait, Edward M. 1927. *American Parties and Elections*. New York: The Century Co.

Schattschneider, E. E. 1942. *Party Government*. New York: Holt, Rinehart and Winston.

Shafer, Bryon E. 1983. *Quiet Revolution*. New York: Russell Sage Foundation.

Southwell, Priscilla L. 1988. Open versus Closed Primaries and Candidate Fortunes, 1972–1984. *American Politics Quarterly* 16:280–95.

Thompson, C. S. 1902. *The Rise and Fall of the Congressional Caucus as a Machine for Nominating Candidates for the Presidency*. New Haven: Yale University Press.

Traugott, Michael. 1985. The Media and the Nominating Process. In *Before Nomination*, edited by George Grassmuck. Washington, D.C.: American Enterprise Institute.

Tufte, Edward. 1973. The Relationship between Seats and Votes in Two Party Systems. *American Political Science Review* 67:540–54.

Verba, Sidney, and Norman H. Nie. 1972. *Participation in America: Political Democracy and Social Equality*. New York: Harper and Row.

Wattenberg, Martin P. 1984. When You Can't Beat Them Join Them: Shaping the Presidential Nominating Process to the Television Age. Paper presented at the annual meeting of the American Political Science Association, Washington, D.C.

Wattier, Mark J. 1983a. The Simple Act of Voting in 1980 Democratic Presidential Primaries. *American Politics Quarterly* 3:267–91.

———. 1983b. Ideological Voting in 1980 Republican Presidential Primaries. *Journal of Politics* 45:1016–26.

————. 1983c. Correlates of Voter Participation in the 1980 Presidential Primaries. Paper presented at the annual meeting of the American Political Science Association, Chicago.

Weaver, David H., Doris A. Graber, Maxwell E. McCombs, and Chaim H. Eyal. 1981. *Media Agenda-Setting in a Presidential Election.* New York: Praeger.

Williams, Daniel C., Stephen J. Weber, Gordon A. Haaland, Ronald H. Mueller, and Robert E. Craig. 1976. Voter Decisionmaking in a Primary Election: An Evaluation of Three Models of Choice. *American Journal of Political Science* 20:37–49.

Wilmerding, Lucius, Jr. 1958. *The Electoral College.* New Brunswick, N.J.: Rutgers University Press.

Wilson, Woodrow. 1911. *Constitutional Government in the United States.* New York: Columbia University Press.

Winograd, Morley. 1978. *Commission on Presidential Nomination and Party Structure, Openness, Participation and Party Building: Reforms for a Stronger Democratic Party.* Washington, D.C.: Democratic National Committee.

Wolfinger, Raymond, and Steven J. Rosenstone. 1980. *Who Votes?* New Haven: Yale University Press.

Index

About the Author

JOHN G. GEER is Assistant Professor of Political Science at Arizona State University, Tempe. He has published in the *American Journal of Political Science, Journal of Politics, Public Opinion Quarterly,* and *American Politics Quarterly*.